BRISTOL
BLENHEIM

1935 to 1944 (all marks)

COVER CUTAWAY: Bristol Blenheim Mk I.
(Mike Badrocke)

First published in July 2015

A catalogue record for this book is available from the British Library.

ISBN 978 0 85733 812 9

Library of Congress control No. 2014956836

Published by Haynes Publishing,
Sparkford, Yeovil,
Somerset BA22 7JJ, UK.
Tel: 01963 442030 Fax: 01963 440001
Int. tel: +44 1963 442030
Int. fax: +44 1963 440001
E-mail: sales@haynes.co.uk
Website: www.haynes.co.uk

Haynes North America Inc.,
861 Lawrence Drive, Newbury Park,
California 91320, USA.

Printed in the USA by Odcombe Press LP,
1299 Bridgestone Parkway, La Vergne,
TN 37086.

Acknowledgements

Gathering the material for this manual would have been impossible without the enthusiastic support of so many. Firstly John Romain, who has allowed the author access to the Blenheim Mk I's restoration over numerous years, and who kindly allowed for an air-to-air photo shoot after one of the aircraft's early air tests to ensure that this book contains pictures of L6739 in flight, which many enthusiasts will be keen to see from its debut air show season.

Also the many contributors whose various inputs and work have given such a great depth to this book. John 'Smudge' Smith for all his knowledge and co-operation; Colin Swann; François Prins for supplying the history of the Blenheim in the East and photos of the Mk I's early restoration; Squadron Leader Dicky James MBE for arranging for the loan of the Blenheim Mk V photo album from 13 Squadron used to show a complete sortie and the behind-the-scenes views; Andy Hay for his superb computer art profile drawings; and finally Anna McDowell, Merill Gilley and Pam Binge at ARC for their hospitality and help during the author's many visits. To all of these, the author offers his grateful thanks.

BRISTOL BLENHEIM

1935 to 1944 (all marks)

Haynes

Owners' Workshop Manual

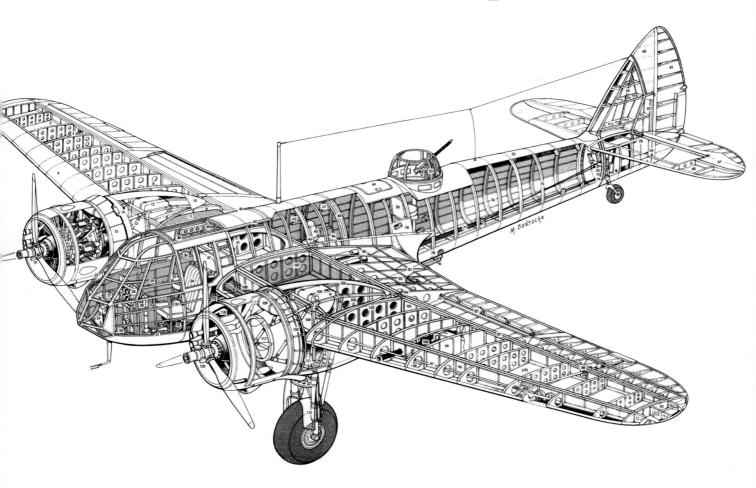

M. Badrocke

An insight into owning, restoring, servicing and flying Britain's
first all-metal monoplane light bomber

Jarrod Cotter

Contents

6 Introduction

Forgotten no more   8

16 The Blenheim story

'Britain First'   19
The Blenheim bomber   22
Blenheims at war   25

40 Restore to flight

Not to be beaten   44
Blenheim rebirth   46

56 Anatomy of the Blenheim

Fuselage   60
Mainplanes   71
Undercarriage   75
Flying controls   79
Engine installation   83
Fuel system   85
Oil system   86
Engine controls   87
Hydraulic system   89
Pneumatic system   89
Armament   91
Oxygen apparatus   93

94 The owner's view

Climbing aboard   96
Start-up   97
Pre-take-off checks   98
Airborne   98
General handling   98
Display routine   99
Landing   99

100 The crew's view

Preliminaries   102
Engine start and warm-up   102
Engine tests   102
Taxying out   103
Take-off   106
After take-off   106
Climbing   107
Cruising   107
General flying   108
Approach and landing   109

128 The engineer's view

152 Appendices

Appendix 1: Bristol Blenheim Mk I
leading particulars   152
Appendix 2: Blenheim production list   155
Appendix 3: RAF Blenheim squadrons   158
Appendix 4: The Blenheim family tree   160
Appendix 5: Foreign service   165
Appendix 6: Glossary and abbreviations   168
Appendix 7: Useful contacts   169

170 Bibliography

171 Index

**OPPOSITE Bristol Blenheim Mk I L6739 basking in some
glorious winter sunshine at Duxford on 3 December 2014.**
(Jarrod Cotter)

'It's unique in the air in that some aircraft look great on the ground and equally nice in the air, but the Blenheim looks astounding in the air and OK on the ground. When you see it flying next to you it takes on a different look. It's got a graceful beauty which it lacks on the ground.'

John Romain, Blenheim Duxford Ltd

Introduction

The Bristol Blenheim holds a very important place in British aviation heritage. When delivered for service with 114 Squadron in early March 1937, it was the RAF's first all-metal monocoque monoplane and became the fastest aircraft on the inventory, and remained as the Service's fastest bomber at the outbreak of the Second World War.

OPPOSITE **A unique sight the world over, as Bristol Blenheim Mk I L6739/YP-Q (G-BPIV) is caught en route back to Duxford following an early air test on 3 December 2014. Not only is this aircraft currently the world's only airworthy Blenheim, it is also the only complete Blenheim in 'short-nose' Mk I configuration. Following a ten-year restoration it first flew in this guise on 20 November 2014.** (Jarrod Cotter)

As the war got underway, the Blenheim and its crews began to suffer heavy losses when faced with overwhelming odds flying at low level in daylight against the latest defences. Consequently, the restoration of a Blenheim to airworthy condition created a great tribute to the brave 'Blenheim Boys', and the aircraft became hugely popular with a worldwide audience. The most recent reincarnation of G-BPIV in Mk IF configuration as a night-fighter variant has also offered later generations the sight of an aircraft not seen flying in Britain since the war – the 'short-nosed' Blenheim. This book tells a far-ranging story of the Blenheim, from its origins as a civilian fast transport, through the maintenance and flying of the type and right up to the recent rebirth of the world's only airworthy example of a truly classic and beautiful British aircraft.

Forgotten no more

For many years the Bristol Blenheim was considered to be one of the 'forgotten bombers', being largely overshadowed by the exploits of the crews of other iconic British types which were developed later, such as the Avro Lancaster and de Havilland Mosquito. However, I'm always surprised at how this situation came about, since the Blenheim was such a revolution as it replaced biplane bombers following its entry into service in 1937 and was a virtual backbone of the RAF in the early years of the Second World War.

The Blenheim was the first all-metal monocoque aircraft that the RAF had ever ordered and it gained many notable accolades. As well as being the RAF's original all-metal monoplane, it was the first aircraft with a monocoque stressed skin construction, a hydraulically operated retractable undercarriage and flaps, and a power turret. When initially tested at A&AEE Martlesham Heath, it was found to be considerably faster than even the RAF's front-line fighters of the time. At the start of the war, Blenheim crews contained much of the cream of the pre-war RAF aircrew, and as well as being used in its intended bomber role, for a time it became the RAF's principal night-fighter. It was also a Blenheim that flew the

BELOW The first Blenheim fitted with full military equipment was Mk I K7037, seen here at Filton in February 1937 shortly before being delivered to 114 Squadron – the first RAF unit to receive the type. *(Bristol)*

first operational sortie of the war over enemy territory. Furthermore, the type flew on front-line operations from the beginning to end of the Second World War, and served in every RAF Command and in every theatre of war. With such an impressive CV – even though it quickly became outclassed and almost obsolete – and when you consider all of its achievements in a time of need, it surprises me that the Blenheim became so overshadowed.

There is no doubt that the work of the Aircraft Restoration Company and its volunteers to restore the first Blenheim to airworthy condition in 1987 brought interest in the aircraft to the fore, being the world's only airworthy example of its type. After the first example was destroyed just a short while later, a prolific number of requests and offers of support led to a second restoration which proved the Blenheim's new-found popularity.

In 2003 a landing accident unfortunately resulted in G-BPIV needing another major restoration. However, instead of returning it to its familiar Mk IV configuration, a decision was made to restore a Blenheim Mk I nose

ABOVE All-over black Blenheim Mk I K7159/YX-N of 54 Operational Training Unit (OTU) aloft over England in 1941. *(Air Ministry)*

BELOW A wintry scene showing an RAF Blenheim Mk IV in France, where the type supported the British Expeditionary Force (BEF) in trying to take the war back to the invading German forces. *(Crown Copyright)*

Blenheim Mk IV R3612/
BL-V of 40 Squadron
captured on camera in
the air during 1940.
(Air Ministry)

RIGHT Former Bristol
employee Ralph
Nelson bought a
surplus Blenheim Mk I
nose and turned
it into this electric
car. He saved all
the components
and material he
removed or cut away
and later donated
it to the Blenheim
project. It has since
been identified as
coming from L6739
and following a
meticulous restoration
is now flying as part of
G-BPIV. *(ARC)*

and fit that to the aircraft. The nose came with considerable provenance, having been taken from a 23 Squadron night-fighter. Therefore, when G-BPIV returned to the air in this new Mk I guise in late November 2014, it offered people the sight of an aircraft not seen in the air since the war.

Following the popular and now-familiar Haynes aircraft manual format, this book shows the Blenheim in a way that I believe has not been possible before. There is a mix of historic and contemporary material illustrating and describing the type and its history, as well as technical information on how it was maintained in service and how the world's only airworthy Blenheim was recently restored and is currently maintained and flown. While some of the photographs used are familiar – though necessarily used because of their specific content – many are little-seen or previously unpublished. These I have sourced from unfamiliar archives containing rare material

– and of course thanks to John Romain's wholehearted support of this book we also include what were the first air-to-airs taken of the newly restored, and the world's only, Bristol Blenheim Mk I.

This book offers the reader an insight into the story behind what many will see flying at UK air shows from 2015. Having been very fortunate to have seen the Blenheim take to the air and even fly alongside it to obtain air-to-air photographs to complete the story of this incredible project, I know that L6739 will bring much pleasure to its audiences in the years to come, and once again pay a fitting tribute to the daring exploits of the brave 'Blenheim Boys'. I hope this piece of work will also honour the heroic Blenheim crews of the Second World War, as well as all those who have given up countless hours so that during the past few decades later generations have been able to see this majestic classic British aircraft take to the skies.

ABOVE The Mk IV nose previously fitted to G-BPIV is on public display in Hangar 3 at the Imperial War Museum (IWM), Duxford. *(Jarrod Cotter)*

It is wonderful enough to see historic aircraft carefully preserved and well presented in a controlled museum environment. Just to look at a combat veteran bomber aircraft in an atmospherically lit museum can be enough to conjure up thoughts of all that its crew went through on a dangerous wartime operation at night, for example. However, for those of us from later generations who might never have seen a particular type flying, the sight and sound of one of those aircraft starting up, taxying out, taking off and then performing a flying demonstration or aerial display brings those aircraft to life.

Therefore, the efforts of those who restore and maintain classic aircraft – be they fragile wood and canvas biplanes of First World War period design or sleek all-metal monoplane fighters from the Second World War – are to be applauded. They keep alive the memories of those who flew and fought in these machines, which while now long since obsolete from the front-line were at the cutting edge of aviation technology in their day.

The Aircraft Restoration Company (ARC) is based in Building 425 at the eastern edge of Duxford, adjacent to the M11, and is one of the largest of the specialist aero engineering companies located at the Cambridgeshire airfield. ARC provides an extensive range of aviation services for aircraft owners. With CAA approvals M3, M5, B1 and E4, ARC has completed many outstanding airworthy restorations. In 2008 the continued expansion and development of the

BELOW The Aircraft Restoration Company's (ARC) Building 425 complex at the eastern extremity of Duxford airfield seen from the air. This building also houses Historic Flying Ltd (HFL), which specialises in the restoration to flight of Supermarine Spitfires. *(Jarrod Cotter)*

business allowed ARC to qualify for the award of the BS EN ISO 9001:2008 systems certification.

John Romain, a former Hawker Siddeley and British Aerospace engineer, is now the Managing Director of the company. As well as being a skilled specialist aero engineer, John is also a hugely respected warbird pilot with a wide variety of types in his logbook, including over 750 hours on the Supermarine Spitfire alone. Nowadays he is one of the world's most experienced warbird pilots on a wide variety of types, and is currently the world's only qualified Blenheim pilot (though well-known Duxford warbird pilot Lee Proudfoot will in due course be passed to fly the aircraft too).

ARC undertakes major servicing and repairs on historic aircraft for a number of warbird owners in the UK and abroad, and in recent years has even secured contracts for the Ministry of Defence, where numerous major servicings of the RAF Battle of Britain Memorial Flight's (BBMF) fighters have been carried out. In the future this will include major servicing on the RAF BBMF's Avro Lancaster and Douglas Dakota too, which ARC is currently preparing for with the construction of a new, larger hangar on its present site.

In the same hangar in recent years numerous world-leading airworthy Supermarine Spitfire restorations have been produced. One of the most notable examples has been Mk I P9374, which was restored to the condition of a very early Spitfire complete with hand-cranked undercarriage. The hangar is, of course, shared by the Aircraft Restoration Company and Historic Flying Limited (HFL).

ARC, or Propshop Ltd which is its formal name, was established at Duxford in 1989 and perhaps became best known for its Bristol Blenheim restorations led by John Romain. The owner of HFL, Karel Bos, had wanted his company to be based at Duxford and so moved there in about 2005. John and Karel then built the new workshop and hangar facility together. The intention was that they would remain as two separate companies, with HFL specialising in the rebuild of Spitfires and ARC operating an 'umbrella' effect on the overall set-up. It all worked extremely well and world-class Spitfires were soon coming off the HFL production line, with ARC carrying out the maintenance and

ABOVE ARC has become synonymous with the operation of the world's only airworthy Blenheim, and hence the type's silhouette appears on the company's logo. *(Jarrod Cotter)*

restoration of a varied array of warbirds and its employees responsible for flying operations.

MoD Contracts

Since 2005 ARC has successfully tendered for Ministry of Defence (MoD) contracts to carry out major maintenance on military-operated aircraft such as the Spitfires and Hurricanes of the BBMF. This aspect of the company's work has recently become more established. They started off as one-off contracts – one Spitfire or one Hurricane – which had to be tendered for separately. After several years working in that way, it became obvious to both ARC and the MoD that it would be far better if a long-term contract was offered. That contract was put up for tender, and ARC was successful in securing it.

Because of the MoD's requirements for quality systems, it was recommended that ARC should get an ISO 9000 accreditation. The company earned an ISO 9001 accreditation in 2009, which was later upgraded to ISO 9007. This was a crucial aspect in obtaining the long-term MoD contracts.

ABOVE Hawker Hurricane Mk IIc PZ865 of the RAF Battle of Britain Memorial Flight – the last Hurricane built – was one of the numerous MoD contract restorations that have been carried out by ARC in its Building 425 workshops. The Second World War fighter is seen here having its Rolls-Royce Merlin engine refitted by ARC engineers. *(Jarrod Cotter)*

The MoD approvals further expanded too, as ARC began the process of going for an MAOS, which is an MoD/military maintenance approval that would enable the company to continue to do MoD work in the years to come. The next step was to work towards gaining the DAOS, which is the design approval. That was needed for the future, with the eventual goal that ARC would become the design centre for the Spitfire and Hurricane.

The next much-anticipated major restoration achievement by ARC will be the return to the skies of Westland Lysander Mk I V9312.

Currently undergoing a major and complex refurbishment, this aircraft was built by Westland during 1940 and subsequently served with 612, 225 and 4 Squadrons, so comes with enormous provenance.

As mentioned, occupying the same hangar as ARC is Historic Flying Ltd, which specialises in the rebuilding of Spitfires. This company is in effect a modern-day 'Spitfire factory', and has in recent years rebuilt two early Spitfire Mk Is. These, complete with their hand-cranked undercarriage system, are of a completely different breed to the Spitfires we have become used to seeing.

All in all, what goes on in Building 425 at Duxford is unique the world over. This book brings you a rare glimpse into the incredible work which goes on there, the most recent example of which is the world's only airworthy Bristol Blenheim, and the only complete Blenheim Mk I.

ABOVE While ARC occupies the southern half of the Building 425 complex, in the northern half is HFL which specialises in the restoration of Spitfires. Among the company's latest accolades are the rare early Mk I Spitfires, two out of three of which have already been returned to the skies. This is N3200, the second of the superb Spitfire Mk I restorations. *(Jarrod Cotter)*

LEFT The imposing reception of Building 425, with a Spitfire impressively embossed on to the front office window. *(Jarrod Cotter)*

'The charge of the Light Brigade at Balaclava is eclipsed in brightness by these almost daily deeds of fame.'

Winston Churchill, British Prime Minister,
talking in August 1941 about the duties carried out
by the RAF's daylight bomber crews

Chapter One

The Blenheim story

Despite not being initially designed as a military requirement, the Bristol Blenheim transformed the pre-war RAF and brought its inventory of aircraft into a new age. It entered RAF service in March 1937, and even with the threatened onset of another major conflict it was still the RAF's fastest bomber when the Second World War broke out in September 1939.

OPPOSITE An original press picture from October 1936 showing Bristol Type 142M K7033, the prototype of the Blenheim bomber. The keen-eyed reader will notice that parts of the aircraft have been hand brushed, including the gap between the rudder and tailfin, the gaps between the ailerons and the wings, and the area below the turret and the port roundel to name but a few. The brushed alterations are noticeable on the original print scanned for this book, which was sourced from the USA. *(Wide World)*

RIGHT Captain Frank Barnwell while he was serving as a pilot in the Royal Flying Corps. He became the Chief Designer of the Bristol Aeroplane Company and among his most successful designs were the Bristol F.2b Fighter and the Blenheim. He was killed in a flying accident on 2 August 1938. *(Bristol)*

RIGHT The 1st Viscount Rothermere, who was the first Secretary of State for Air and the proprietor of the *Daily Mail*. It was he who ordered the high-speed Bristol Type 142 for potential use by his journalists and photographers to get to breaking stories around Europe quickly, but due to its military potential donated it to the nation. He named it 'Britain First' and it formed the basis for the revolutionary design of the Blenheim. Lord Rothermere died on 26 November 1947, aged 72. *(Crown Copyright)*

Blenheims suffered heavy losses flying in the hostile daylight bombing role, but they remained a backbone of the RAF until the rapid design advances of a wartime environment brought more capable aircraft into the conflict to replace it. The Blenheim holds a key place in British aviation heritage and its story deserves to be told as a fitting tribute to all those who risked and lost their lives flying this once revolutionary aircraft.

It was in early 1933 that the Bristol Aeroplane Company's designer Frank Barnwell began the process of designing a civilian light transport aircraft which would be capable of cruising at around 250mph, powered by Bristol's forthcoming new Aquila engines. By that summer, Barnwell and his team had drawn up a design for an all-metal, twin-engined, low-wing monoplane capable of carrying six passengers, originally given the name 'Bristol Type No 135'.

In early 1934 the 1st Viscount Rothermere, who had formerly been the Secretary of State for Air and was by then the proprietor of the *Daily Mail* newspaper, held an aviation-themed meeting for his editors. The *Daily Mail* had a history of supporting aviation by offering large monetary prizes for achievements such as the first crossing of the Channel, and Lord Rothermere asked his editors to promote the advantages that new civil aircraft designs were bringing to the business world by offering faster, more efficient transport. He was a keen advocate of the British aviation industry and, during the meeting, had expressed a wish to have his own 'executive' aircraft which could fly journalists and photographers to the locations of breaking stories anywhere in Europe at short notice and quickly. Robert T. Lewis, editor of the *Bristol Evening World* (which was part of the *Daily Mail* and Associated Newspapers Group owned by Lord Rothermere), was aware of the Type 135 idea and informed Lord Rothermere of this ongoing project to design a fast transport aircraft at Bristol's Filton Works. The design met his requirements perfectly; however, it would be held up as the Aquila had not even been bench tested at this time.

Therefore, as a delay was out of the question, Frank Barnwell looked at the option of replacing the proposed Aquilas with a pair of supercharged Bristol Mercury engines. After making his performance recalculations, Barnwell announced that this redesign would result in an aircraft still capable of 240mph. The aircraft was given the new name 'Bristol Type No 142'.

Yet, this fast transport could have placed Bristol in a dilemma. Obviously the Air Ministry was the company's biggest customer, and the RAF of the mid-1930s didn't even have a fighter capable of achieving such a top cruising speed, so there were concerns by senior board members at Bristol that it could cause embarrassment to the Air Ministry. Consequently, to keep the officials appeased,

Bristol approached the Air Ministry before going ahead with the deal, and after approval from such key figures as Air Marshal Sir Hugh Dowding and Viscount Trenchard, it was decided that Lord Rothermere's aircraft could be built, powered by two 650hp Bristol Mercury VI S.2 nine-cylinder air-cooled radial engines. Its cost would be £18,500, half payable in advance and half on completion of the aircraft's build in 12 months. Bristol also began the development of a private venture version of the aircraft, the Type 143, which would be powered by the company's new 500hp Aquila radial engines once they were in production.

'Britain First'

Having been allocated the civil registration G-ADCZ but actually only wearing the experimental registration R-12, the Type 142 performed its maiden flight at Filton on 12 April 1935, initially fitted with fixed-pitch four-bladed wooden propellers and flown by Bristol's Chief Test Pilot Cyril Uwins. The aircraft had looked sleek and impressive enough on the ground with its polished metal finish, but once in the air and with its wheels retracted, it immediately appeared even more impressive. Even with the wooden propellers the Type 142 performed superbly, but a month later these were replaced with metal three-bladed, variable-pitch Hamilton Standards, which Lord

Rothermere had imported from the USA. These not only improved the aircraft's take-off and climb performance, but its top speed soon exceeded 300mph.

Lord Rothermere was delighted with these figures, perhaps in part because his business rival Lord Beaverbrook, proprietor of the *Daily Express*, had recently acquired a Lockheed 12 Electra which was around 100mph slower than the Type 142! However, more importantly, his support of British aviation must have given him immense pride that Bristol had produced, at his request, this world-leading aircraft.

ALL METAL AIRCRAFT OF OUTSTANDING PERFORMANCE.
Fitted with "Bristol" Mercury Engines.

"Britain First"

"Bristol"
TYPE 142
THE BRISTOL AEROPLANE CO., LTD., FILTON, BRISTOL

ABOVE A view of Bristol Type 142 K7557 wearing the No 5 at Hendon for display in the New Types Park at the RAF Display of June 1936. Prototype Blenheim K7033 had been due to appear there, but following a flap failure during a landing K7557 was sent as a replacement. *(No 101 Squadron Archives)*

LEFT A period advertisement for the Bristol Type 142 'Britain First' as published in June 1936. *(Bristol)*

ABOVE An original postcard from 1935 showing Bristol Type 142 K7557 'Britain First' flying in an atmospheric skyscape. (Real Photo Postcard)

This situation caused some controversy, as the latest RAF fighter just ordered into production – the Gloster Gladiator – was around 40mph slower than the Type 142! Obviously the Air Ministry took note of the Type 142's performance, and offered to allow it to go to the Aeroplane & Armament Experimental Establishment (A&AEE) at Martlesham Heath for trials. The aircraft was given the military serial number K7557 and proudly wore RAF roundels. The Service pilots were delighted with the Type 142's performance, and when it is considered that they had only recently completed the testing of the Boulton Paul Overstrand, a twin-engined, fabric-covered biplane bomber with a fixed undercarriage and only capable of reaching 148mph, it is hardly surprising that they were impressed at the prospect of a military machine of similar design and performance to the Type 142. It had flown very well at Martlesham, attaining a top speed with a full payload of 285mph, and a maximum speed of 307mph.

The Air Ministry held a meeting in July 1935 at which Frank Barnwell showed drawings for the Type 142M – the 'M' standing for Military. The Air Ministry officials were convinced and issued a new specification for a medium bomber – Specification 28/35. Lord Rothermere was such a keen advocate of British air superiority, that realising the aircraft's potential he named the Type 142 'Britain First' and gifted it to the nation. Sir Philip Cunliffe-Lister, Secretary of State for Air, sent him a telegraph stating the following: 'Lord Rothermere, c/o *Daily Mail*, London. On behalf of the Air Council, I gratefully accept your generous offer.'

However, how all this was reported at the time highlights that the full story of the aircraft's development was yet to be made widely public. *The Aeroplane* of 21 August 1935, stated:

LEFT Boulton Paul Overstrand J9179 of 101 Squadron. When it is considered that the Service pilots at Martlesham Heath had just completed the testing of this cumbersome biplane bomber with fixed undercarriage, and with fabric-covered wings, just how revolutionary the Type 142's design was at the time can really be appreciated. (101 Squadron Archives)

Everybody barring of course the Pacifists and the Little Englanders, will be heartily glad to hear of Lord Rothermere's latest gift to the British nation – the twin-motored monoplane which was built by the Bristol Aeroplane Co Ltd.

We were, naturally, under a vow of secrecy about its calculated performance before it was produced, and its actual performance since it has been tested at Martlesham has not been published. The statement has been made that its speed is 270mph, but that is not, so far as we can discover, an official figure. And we should hate to shock our friends in America by claiming for a British twin-engined transport machine a performance which has not already been surpassed in the United States. At the same time we believe that the machine is in fact a great deal faster than anything in the States except pure racing machines.

The original machine, as seen at the Paris Show, was definitely intended to be a high-speed commercial machine, whereas, according to the reported conversation between Lord Rothermere and 'the chief aerial engineering firms in Britain', Lord Rothermere's idea was a high-speed bomber. So the question arises whether the original design was that of Captain Barnwell and the Bristol Co for a high-speed transport machine, of which we have heard more or less by gossip for about 18 months, or whether it was entirely Lord Rothermere's conception put into practical form by Captain Barnwell and the Bristol Co. But the point is hardly worth arguing in detail because it is so much like the argument whether the hen or egg came first.

The fact remains that whether the machine is fitted with seats for passengers or racks for bombs we definitely have a high-powered transport machine which seems to be rather faster than anything in the World, whether measured by its sheer top speed or by what we should call its operational cruising speed. …

Work on the Type 142 was the priority, and the Type 143 became rapidly overshadowed. Its Aquila engines were not ready until late 1935, and once again it was Cyril Uwins who flew this aircraft on its maiden flight from Filton, which took place on 20 January 1936. This

ABOVE Bristol Type 142 K7557 'Britain First' on short finals for landing at Hendon during the 1936 RAF Display. *(Rex/Associated Newspapers)*

ABOVE The Bristol Type 143 G-ADEK, seen with its Bristol Aquila engines being ground run at Filton. *(Bristol)*

BELOW A rare picture showing the Type 142 K7557 while it was on secondment to 101 Squadron. This unit was an established bomber unit that was flying the Boulton Paul Overstrand, an example of which can be seen in the background. *(101 Squadron Archives)*

ABOVE Prototype Bristol Blenheim Mk I K7033 seen at Martlesham Heath while undergoing Service evaluation trials. *(British Official)*

The Blenheim bomber

Although obviously there were many design differences between the Type 142 and Type 142M, perhaps of most significance was that the 142M's wing was raised by about 16in to a more mid-wing position on the fuselage, rather than being of low-wing configuration, and was positioned in order to allow for the placement of an internal bomb bay underneath the fuselage. It also included a dorsal turret for defence, but retained its Mercury engine fit. The first-built Type 142M, K7033, introduced the name Blenheim to this breed of modern aircraft and so the now-familiar workhorse bomber was born. This prototype performed its maiden flight on 25 June 1936, and was sent to Boscombe Down for trials and evaluation on 27 October that year. The type was given final approval for entry to service in December 1936.

aircraft never left Filton, though, and becoming registered G-ADEK it was used as a test-bed for the Aquila engine until that project was abandoned. The Type 143 was consequently scrapped by 1940.

Meanwhile, the Type 142 continued its trials and was modified by Bristol before going to the Royal Aircraft Establishment for further trials in April 1936. It was also seconded to 24 Squadron, a training unit, and then to 101 Squadron, an established bomber unit which was flying the Boulton Paul Overstrand. K7557 had soon fulfilled its task and with the focus switching to the Type 142M lost much of its prominence and was grounded by 1942. It saw out its days at 10 School of Technical Training, and was damaged by an enemy bomb before being scrapped in 1944.

The Blenheim Mk I was fitted with two Bristol Mercury VIIIs, rated at 840hp. Its top speed with a full load was quoted as 279mph at 15,000ft and the maximum speed in excess of 300mph. Its climb rate with a full load was 1,360ft per minute, the Blenheim taking 8.8 minutes to reach 15,000ft. The service ceiling was 30,000ft.

BELOW The prototype Bristol Blenheim Mk I K7033 seen having lost its bare metal finish in favour of camouflage paintwork, *c*1939. Note also that the aircraft is still fitted with propeller spinners, not a feature on the main production aircraft. *(Bristol)*

RIGHT A period advertisement from March 1937, clearly stating that despite its civilian origins the Blenheim was a bomber aircraft. *(Bristol)*

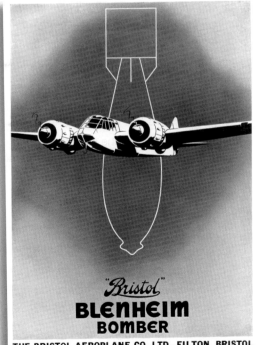

"Bristol"
BLENHEIM
BOMBER
THE BRISTOL AEROPLANE CO. LTD., FILTON, BRISTOL

The first delivery of the Blenheim Mk I to the RAF was made to 114 Squadron under the command of Squadron Leader Hugh Hamilton-Brookes on 1 March 1937, when three Blenheims arrived at Wyton, Cambridgeshire. K7035 was the first to arrive, and this Blenheim had been modified into one of the very few dual-control trainers, so that squadron pilots could be converted from their single-engined Hawker Hind and Audax biplanes to the new multi-engined monoplane. A few days later K7036, K7037 and K7038 arrived.

Having flown biplanes for numerous years, the pre-war RAF bomber pilots took a while to get used to this new and very modern design, which was of course not only an entirely different form of aircraft to become familiar with, but was also considerably faster than anything they had flown before. It was therefore likely that an accident might happen soon. ...

On 10 March, one of the squadron's pilots had made his landing in K7036, and as he rolled down Wyton's runway, gave the aircraft's powerful hydraulic brakes rather too much pressure – the tail quickly went up into the air, and before the pilot could do anything to correct his error the Blenheim's propellers chewed into the ground, forcing the aircraft over and on to its back. The aircraft was damaged beyond repair and was struck off charge a few months later. Accidents such as this were commonplace during this period as the pilots learned to cope with more power, more speed and the rather more complicated handling of high-powered asymmetrics.

That year's RAF Display on 26 June 1937 at Hendon in London featured some of 114 Squadron's Blenheims as the star attraction. The type featured on the poster and programme cover, and the public had its first chance to view a Blenheim up close on the ground. In the air three Blenheims in formation impressed the huge crowd with a low pass over the airfield.

By the year's end four more units had been equipped with the Blenheim, as 44, 90, 139 and 144 Squadrons joined No 114 in converting to the type. Blenheim production had gathered pace by early 1938, and the obsolete biplanes were rapidly withdrawn from operational squadrons to be replaced with this fast monoplane bomber.

In late September 1938 the infamous 'Munich Crisis', caused by a settlement agreement permitting Nazi Germany to forcibly take over portions of Czechoslovakia along the country's borders, threatened to begin another major war in Europe. At this time 16 home-based RAF units were flying Blenheims, and 30 Squadron at Habbanya in Iraq had become the first to operate the type overseas.

However, even prior to the threatening climate created by the 'Munich Crisis' the Blenheim Mk I was already seen to be becoming outdated, as the new generation of high-performance single-seat fighters was constantly developing improvements. In Germany the Messerschmitt Bf 109 was capable of a maximum speed of well over

ABOVE **A very nicely flown port echelon formation of three Blenheim Mk Is of 114 Squadron, which was the first RAF unit to receive the type in March 1937.** *(Crown Copyright)*

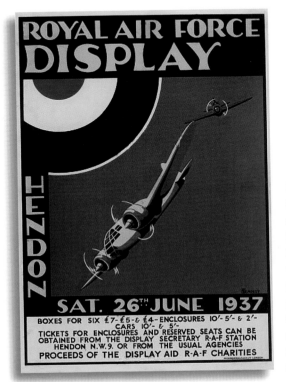

LEFT **On Saturday 26 June 1937, a star attraction at the RAF Display were three Blenheim Mk Is from 114 Squadron, which performed formation passes over the huge crowds, showing off the Service's new bomber.** *(Crown Copyright)*

300mph, highlighting the fact that the less agile Blenheim would be vulnerable in a hostile engagement with such an aircraft.

The Mk IV

Several countries had been sold the Blenheim Mk I, some of which expressed a desire for a longer-range variant with a faster top speed. After a meeting with Canadian technicians, Frank Barnwell issued a design specification for the Type 149, which among its improvements over the Mk I featured fuel tanks in the outer wing sections and a lengthened nose to improve the navigator/bomb-aimer's working environment. Specification 11/36 was subsequently issued by the Air Ministry, and this variant was renamed the Bolingbroke. The prototype was K7072, which was a modified Mk I featuring similar glazing to the original, but which was lengthened. Cyril Uwins first flew this aircraft on 24 September 1937, but was critical of the windscreen being some 6ft in front of him. This view was shared by other pilots, and so a complete redesign of the nose section was initiated.

By the late spring of 1938 K7072 had been fitted with the new asymmetric 'scalloped' Mk IV nose. This featured a stepped windscreen closer to the pilot, with the port side of the forward glazing recessed to allow him a less obstructed view forward. K7072 went to Martlesham Heath for trials in July 1938, and became the prototype Blenheim Mk IV. (The name Bolingbroke was retained only for the licence-built aircraft later produced in Canada.)

TOP The prototype Blenheim Mk IV K7072 while fitted with the original nose section which retained the profile of the glazing on the Mk I but was extended forward. *(Bristol)*

ABOVE Blenheim Mk IV prototype K7072 in its redesigned form with the new nose that featured scalloped glazing. *(Bristol)*

BELOW Mark IV L4842 shows off the graceful beauty of the Blenheim in flight while being flown by Bristol Test Pilot Bill Pegg on a Bristol publicity flight near Filton on 29 May 1939. The aircraft went on to serve with 53 Squadron and was shot down over France on 17 May 1940. *(Bristol)*

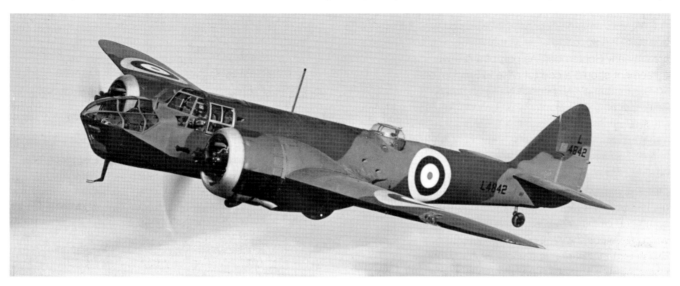

The first production Blenheim Mk IV built was L4823, and the first Mk IVs entered service with 53 Squadron at Odiham, Hampshire, in January 1939.

Blenheims at war

On 3 September 1939, the Second World War was declared. On that day the first RAF aircraft to fly over Germany during the conflict was Blenheim Mk IV N6215 of 139 Squadron. It was flown by Flying Officer Andrew McPherson on an armed reconnaissance sortie to record German warships at the naval base at Wilhelmshaven.

The following day, Blenheim Mk IVs from 107 and 110 Squadrons set out from Wattisham to attack German warships in Heligoland Bight. All ten Blenheims each carried two 500lb semi-armour-piercing bombs, and while some damage was caused to shipping, five of the Blenheims failed to return.

This substantial loss percentage was a very early indication of the dangers of daylight bombing, and Vickers Wellington and Handley Page Hampden crews were to suffer similarly. Unescorted, these relatively low-performance bombers, clearly visible both from the ground and in the air, soon accrued unsustainable losses at the hands of an efficient enemy air defence system.

To France

The RAF Advanced Air Striking Force (AASF) was formed on 24 August 1939 from 1 Group, and its ten squadrons of Fairey Battle light bombers embarked to airfields in the Rheims area in early September. As part of a pre-war agreement should a conflict arise in Europe, on 10 September 1939 the British Expeditionary Force (BEF), consisting of some 158,000 men, left for France.

The AASF was an independent command from the British Expeditionary Force and at first reported directly to the Air Ministry. However, this arrangement proved to be inadequate and on 15 January 1940, it was placed under the command of the British Air Forces in France, which also took the Air Component of the British Expeditionary Force under its command. It was Air Vice Marshal Sir Arthur Sheridan

ABOVE An early war low-level photograph taken during an attack by Blenheim Mk IVs on an enemy convoy sailing between Ijmuiden and The Hague off the Dutch coast. During this action eight vessels, including the MV *Delaware* visible here, were bombed by Blenheims from 105 and 139 Squadrons. Although some bombs hit the ships, three Blenheims were shot down and two crash-landed on return to their base. *(Crown Copyright)*

Barratt KCB CMG MC (later Air Chief Marshal, and nicknamed 'Ugly') who commanded the British Air Forces in France.

Four Blenheim units were sent overseas to join the forces in France, when Nos 18, 53, 114 and 139 were deployed. They were joined by Blenheims of 59 Squadron, which was tasked with night-time reconnaissance sorties over the BEF's front line. Due to a lack of any major offensive operations by either side, this early period of the conflict became known as the

BELOW Groundcrew at Bétheniville servicing the starboard engine of a Bristol Blenheim Mk IV of 139 Squadron, covered with camouflage netting and snow, during the winter of 1939/40. *(Crown Copyright)*

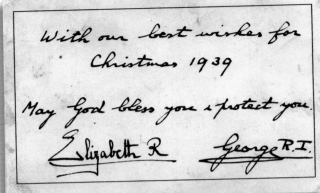

ABOVE A postcard sent by HM King George VI and Queen Elizabeth (better known to later generations as the Queen Mother) to RAF personnel serving in France during Christmas 1939. *(Crown Copyright)*

ABOVE Three Blenheim Mk IVs of 59 Squadron take off from Poix during the Battle of France. *(Crown Copyright)*

'Phoney War' by the British, and the 'Sitzkrieg' (Sitting War) by the Germans. On 10 May 1940, eight months after war had been declared, German troops advanced through Europe, marking the end of the 'Phoney War'. The Battle of France was about to begin.

As soon as the German offensive began, the

RIGHT Riggers inspect the exit holes of enemy machine-gun fire on the fuselage of Blenheim Mk IV N6207/ VE-G of 110 Squadron, while it was under repair at Wattisham, Suffolk, in May 1940. *(Crown Copyright)*

Blenheims began to suffer heavy losses, though more during bombing raids while on the ground at their forward airfields than through being shot down in the air. For example, at 05:45hrs on 11 May, 114 Squadron's base at Condé/Vreux was attacked by nine Dornier Do 17Zs, and six of the unit's Blenheim Mk IVs were destroyed on the ground.

However, on 14 May the squadron pooled its resources from what aircraft it had remaining and sent two Blenheims out on an armed reconnaissance sortie. After attacking an enemy transport column, one of 114 Squadron's Blenheims, L9464, was shot down with all three crew killed. That aircraft was one of 47 light/ medium bombers lost that day, comprising 14 Blenheims and 33 Battles. Another example of the continuing heavy losses occurred on 17 May, when a force of 12 Blenheims attacked enemy tanks and troops near Gembloux – ten were shot down by fighters and another by ground fire.

By 19 May the rapid German advance posed a great threat to the remaining RAF aircraft in theatre. With the Blenheims having sustained heavy losses, the remnants of the squadrons withdrew over the next few days and made their way back to England to regroup. Fighter operations over the battlefield were flown by Hawker Hurricanes and Supermarine Spitfires based in southern England.

Following the falls of Calais and Boulogne, Dunkirk remained the only large port facility available for the evacuation of Allied troops from France. During the evacuation of Dunkirk, codenamed Operation Dynamo, a total of 32 RAF squadrons provided air cover, and with the Battle squadrons having been virtually decimated in France, Blenheim units took over nearly all the RAF's light bomber operations during and in the aftermath of Dunkirk. On 3 June 1940, the last day of Operation Dynamo, the RAF flew 171 reconnaissance, 651 bombing and 2,739 fighter sorties. During the previous nine days, the RAF had lost 177 aircraft.

Fighter variant and the Battle of Britain

Even following the introduction of the Hurricane and Spitfire, with the Blenheim's speed still prominent in the minds of the officials at the Air Ministry, it was decided early on that the type could be modified to be made suitable as a long-range day fighter, which could also be used for night intruder sorties. Designated as the Blenheim Mk IF, the new variant first arrived on 23 and 25 Squadrons in December 1938. It differed from the bomber in that it was fitted with a substantial gun pack in the area of the bomb bay, manufactured by the Ashford workshops of the Southern Railway Company and containing four Browning 0.303in machine guns. The single 0.303in Browning was retained in the port wing and the Lewis 0.303in machine gun was also left in place in the Bristol dorsal turret. The added drag of the Mk IF's gun pack reduced its top speed by nearly 30mph, leaving it much slower than the new monoplane fighters which were now entering service both with the RAF and the Luftwaffe.

Over 200 Blenheims were converted to fighter standard and, at the outbreak of the war, 111 of them were serving with Fighter Command. During the early months, many Blenheims were lost in daylight operations, causing great concern to Fighter Command. So before June 1940, with France having fallen, a decision was made to transfer all of Fighter Command's Blenheim fighter squadrons to the night-fighting role. It had become obvious that the Blenheim IF's performance was no match for the Messerschmitt Bf 109, but it could be used more effectively at night. Simultaneously, the type was selected as the most suitable for the testing of airborne radar and this ground-breaking technology first found success with Blenheims.

Equipped with the Airborne Interception (AI) Mk IIIm, early trials at night revealed that it was difficult to even find any enemy bombers, let alone engage them. It was 25 Squadron that was

the first unit to operationally trial the new radar while still maintaining its night-fighter role. For this task, the squadron had a flight of AI-equipped Blenheim Mk IVFs, one of the few units in Fighter Command to operate this mark. The majority of these sorties took place over the slightly less hostile environment of the North Sea.

From the beginning of the war, a handful of 23 Squadron Blenheim Mk IFs, based at Collyweston in Northamptonshire, a satellite station close to Wittering in Lincolnshire, were also deployed to Digby further east in the county where they were placed on night readiness. The unit saw little action until the Luftwaffe mounted its first large-scale night raid against British targets on the night of 18/19 June 1940.

So it was that on that night 23 Squadron became the first Blenheim Mk IF unit to achieve success at night, when seven Blenheim Mk IFs were sent on patrol in the area of The Wash. Three Heinkel He 111s were shot down during a raid on London, including 5J+DM which crashed into shallows just off Blakeney on the north Norfolk coast.

This He 111 had fallen victim to the guns of Flight Lieutenant Raymond Duke-Woolley's Blenheim. While flying over Sutton Bridge he had spotted one of his colleagues being shot down by the enemy bomber shortly before midnight on 18 June. His subsequent combat report recorded the incident as such:

Observed a ball of fire, which I took to be a Blenheim fighter in flames, breaking away from behind the tail of the E/A [enemy aircraft]. I climbed to engage the E/A and attacked from below the tail after searchlights were extinguished. I closed to a range of 50 yards

ABOVE Pilot Officer Peter Kells climbs into the cockpit of his 29 Squadron Blenheim Mk IF for a night patrol from Coleby Grange, Lincolnshire, in October 1940. *(Crown Copyright)*

and opened fire. The E/A returned fire and appeared to throttle back suddenly. My own speed was 130–140mph and I estimate the E/A slowed to 110mph. I delivered five attacks with the front guns and during these my air gunner fired seven bursts at various ranges.

After the last front gun attack my air gunner reported that the E/A's port engine was on fire. As my starboard engine was now U/S, I broke off the engagement and returned to base, where several bullet holes were found in the wings and fuselage, including cannon strikes in the starboard wing and rear fuselage.

As Flight Lieutenant Duke-Woolley had not seen the bomber crash, he initially claimed it as a 'probable'. But, it was later confirmed that it had crash-landed in shallow water off Blakeney where its crew had waded ashore and were subsequently captured.

Meanwhile, 23 Squadron's Commanding Officer, Squadron Leader Joseph O'Brien, spotted another He 111 in searchlights close to Newmarket at 01:25hrs on 19 June. Once again the Blenheim pilot flew a number of passes of the German bomber, firing bursts from the front guns, and as the enemy aircraft appeared to the gunner in the rear turret he fired with his Lewis gun. Smoke was seen pouring out of the Heinkel before it disappeared out of sight in a diving turn, seemingly out of control.

Yet, as hinted at already, the successes that night came at a price to 23 Squadron. Two of the seven Blenheims were shot down with three of the aircrew on board them killed, and one of those lost was Squadron Leader O'Brien's L8687/YP-X. Having sent the enemy aircraft earthwards, the pilot quickly lost all control of his Blenheim, which went into a spin. He ordered his crew to bale out, and he and his navigator escaped through the hatch. The air gunner, though, was killed.

No 23 Squadron also acted as an operational testing unit for the new AI radar, carrying out calibration work for the many new ground radar stations which were appearing up and down the country.

As the Luftwaffe had consolidated its squadrons in northern France, more and more frequent attacks on Britain were mounted with

the objective being an eventual invasion of England. But first air superiority needed to be gained, and during the summer of 1940 RAF fighters were put on the front line of a crucial fight for survival. On 10 July 1940, the first phase of the Battle of Britain began.

Such was the importance of the new airborne radar, that the Fighter Interception Unit (FIU) was formed within 11 Group Fighter Command based at Tangmere, Sussex. Continuous testing of the AI Mk III was being carried out and, on the night of 22/23 July 1940, Flying Officer G. Ashfield and his crew of Radar Operator Sergeant R.H. Leyland and Observer Pilot Officer G.E. Morris took off from Tangmere for an interception of enemy aircraft. The system worked well as Ashfield's Blenheim was vectored directly towards a Do 17, which was shot down into the sea off Brighton. The FIU had achieved the world's first successful controlled interception, which had led to the destruction of an enemy aircraft.

Another unit that had a long association with the Blenheim Mk IF was 604 (County of Middlesex) Squadron, with which the Blenheim had been on strength since January 1939. After several moves, the squadron arrived at Middle Wallop in Hampshire on 27 July 1940, where AI radar was installed. Testing had to take place during the afternoons while operational sorties were flown at night looking for prey along the south coast. A success finally came on 11 August when, after a lengthy pursuit, a Heinkel He 59 was set on fire off the French coast. This small victory was tarnished on 15 August. First came the loss of L6610, which was pounced upon by the Spitfires of 609 Squadron during a patrol. Luckily, the crew managed to make it back to Middle Wallop airfield where all survived without injury after the crash-landing, although the aircraft had to be written off. The second blow of the day came when the airfield was bombed by Junkers Ju 88s, which were successful in destroying Blenheim Mk IF L6723.

Following the achievement of the FIU interception, contact with the enemy was few and far between, but 219 Squadron, based at Catterick in Yorkshire, began operating in daylight again on 15 August. The unit really had little choice as it was working alone while the local Hurricane squadrons had been moved south to bolster 11 Group. Entering into its first aerial combat of the war, the squadron managed to claim a Dornier Do 17 'damaged' and a Junkers Ju 88 'probable', all in the face of overwhelming odds.

No 29 Squadron, operating from Debden, Essex, had already opened its account by shooting down two enemy aircraft on 18 June, although this had come at the price of two of their own. A move to Lincolnshire saw the squadron enter a very busy and successful August with a pair of Heinkel He 111s destroyed. A third He 111 was claimed as damaged, but the loss of L1330 and its crew was suffered on 25 August. It was shot down by an unknown enemy aircraft off Wainfleet and more losses were to follow.

It was not until September 1940 that 25 Squadron, which had been flying the Blenheim Mk IF since December 1938, saw its first action. It was action it could well have done without though, because once again, some of the RAF fighter pilots' aircraft recognition skills had failed them. While on patrol over North Weald on 3 September, L1512 was attacked by a Hurricane and shot down, killing the pilot Pilot Officer D.W. Hogg, who had no time to escape the stricken aircraft. This tragic error was quickly erased from the squadron's memory when two He 111s were shot down over Suffolk the following day. Before the month was out, a Do 17 was added to the tally.

No 600 (City of London) Squadron had been having a difficult time with its AI-equipped Blenheims and since suffering heavy losses in May 1940 had been confined to the night-fighting role. Contact with the enemy had been negligible, although a Heinkel He 59 was damaged on 20 July. Several airfield moves had not helped, combined with very unreliable equipment which left 600 Squadron claiming a single Ju 88 destroyed on 15/16 September during the entire Battle of Britain.

The Blenheim Mk IF could not be classed as a complete success during the Battle of Britain, but had provided a valuable stepping stone for future AI-equipped aircraft. Losses inflicted far outweighed the total enemy aircraft shot down, but the aircraft filled a gap that was seriously lacking in Fighter Command's capability at the time.

ABOVE AND BELOW A series of three photos showing Blenheim Mk IF ZK-X of 25 Squadron making a 'scramble' take-off from an airfield in Suffolk during 1940. *(Crown Copyright)*

Light bombing duties

Meanwhile, from Dunkirk onwards, Blenheim bomber units took over almost all of the RAF's light bombing duties and had been in action throughout the Battle of Britain bombing Luftwaffe airfields by day and night. Although often successful in their duties, the by then outclassed Blenheims suffered further heavy losses.

Blenheims were also involved in the RAF's 'Circus' operations. These were flown to try to draw Luftwaffe fighters into action by sending a small bomber force out as a potential target, with a large fighter escort waiting for the German aircraft to take the bait. The first 'Circus' operation was flown on 10 January 1941, when 114 Squadron sent six Blenheims to bomb an ammunition dump south of Calais, with more than 70 RAF fighters waiting for enemy aircraft to be sent up to attack the bombers.

In early 1941 shipping losses were also becoming unsustainable, so some Blenheim units were temporarily detached from 2 Group Bomber Command to Coastal Command, with which they flew convoy escort, anti-submarine and anti-shipping sorties. Once back with 2 Group, anti-shipping and other maritime sorties continued through the year until November, and yet again the Blenheim crews suffered heavy losses. Some 139 Blenheims had been lost during the aircraft's anti-shipping campaign.

'Bomber' Harris arrives

Air Marshal Sir Arthur Travers Harris was promoted to Commander-in-Chief of Bomber

Command from 22 February 1942. Harris is well known for shaping Bomber Command into an efficient force with war-winning capabilities, and even from his earliest days in this post the Blenheim was not part of his primary plans. On arrival Harris had on strength 78 light bombers (including 56 Blenheims), 309 medium bombers (mostly Vickers Wellingtons) and 69 heavy bombers (Handley Page Halifaxes and Short Stirlings).

In Harris's *Despatches on War Operations 1942–1945*, he commented:

The Light Bomber Force of No 2 Group was also included in my Command at the time. With the exception of night intruder activity against enemy airfields to assist the heavy and medium bombers (and also to hinder the enemy bombers) this short-range force could play no part in the main offensive against Germany. In daylight operations, executed in conjunction with offensive fighter sweeps, the chief purpose of the light bombers was to bring the enemy fighters into combat.

OTUs and the '1,000-bomber' raids

While the Blenheim was on draw-down from operational front-line duties in Europe, as more capable twin-engined bombers arrived, the type played a pivotal role with Operational Training Units. The Blenheim was used to train pilots, navigators, air gunners, bomb-aimers and wireless operators who would go on to fly in the new twins and the latest heavy bomber coming on stream – the seven-man-crewed Avro Lancaster.

Bomber Harris's first '1,000-bomber' raid was Operation Millennium, flown on the night of 30/31 May 1942. This saw 1,047 heavy bombers fly to Cologne, and acting in support of them were aircraft flying on night intruder sorties to enemy night-fighter airfields. The intruders included 49 Blenheims. The second '1,000-bomber' raid was held two nights later, when the target was Essen. Again, some 60 Blenheims supported the heavies.

However, by the time of the third '1,000-bomber' raid, on 25/26 June with the target being Bremen, having lost 70 bombers and with many more damaged on

RIGHT A Blenheim Mk IV of 107 Squadron RAF observes a British oil tanker on fire and sinking in the English Channel after a German attack while on a maritime patrol, c1940. *(Crown Copyright)*

the previous two operations, Harris could not muster sufficient heavies. He therefore used 79 day bombers as part of the raid, which included 51 Blenheims. Also, another 31 Blenheims flew on the more familiar night intruder support duties.

Blenheims in the East

In 1938 the first overseas unit to be equipped with the Blenheim Mk I was 30 Squadron based in Iraq. They had arrived by sea in crates from Sealand via the aircraft depot at Aboukir in late 1937. Once the aircraft had been unpacked and assembled, Vokes tropical air filters were fitted to the carburettor intakes, machine guns were installed and they were then air tested. Deliveries to 30 Squadron at Mosul commenced in January 1938.

This was an important aircraft to the RAF and the fact that it was sent to the Middle East where rather older types (30 Squadron replaced the Hawker Hardy with Blenheims) held sway is an interesting point. Guarding the Suez Canal was paramount and modern aircraft were essential if the RAF was to carry out the task effectively. At this stage in 1938, it was Italy that was a possible nuisance in the area and not (yet) Nazi Germany. Other units were scheduled to receive the Blenheim, but it was not until February and March 1939 that another 50 crated examples arrived; these went to 55 and 84 Squadrons – replacing the Vickers

LEFT Although the Blenheim was not part of 'Bomber' Harris's future plans for the bombing offensive he envisaged, the type was involved in the support of his '1,000-bomber' raids. However, on the third of these, which took place on the night of 25/26 June 1942, to make up the numbers of the 'heavies' lost on the previous two raids, Blenheims were used to bomb the target of Bremen. This advertisement from June 1942 depicted Blenheims bombing an aircraft factory at Bremen. *(Bristol)*

ABOVE As the war progressed and more efficient aircraft replaced it on the front line, the Blenheim became an important aircraft in the training role. Here Mk IV R3607/FV-E of 13 OTU is seen as part of a three-aircraft formation in 1943. *(Crown Copyright)*

BELOW The chocks are seen being removed from Blenheim Mk I L6670 UQ-R of 211 Squadron at Menidi-Tatoi, Greece, in 1941. Note the Vokes tropical air filters fitted to the carburettor intakes beneath the aircraft's engines. *(Crown Copyright)*

Vincent – and a month later 211 Squadron exchanged its Hawker Hinds for Blenheims. Vickers Wellesleys, Westland Wapatis and even Short Singapore flying-boats were replaced with the Blenheim, which was much faster than any of its predecessors.

Desert war

The outbreak of the Second World War on 3 September 1939 did not affect the Middle East immediately; it was only after the fall of France and when Italy declared war on Britain on 10 June 1940, that the situation altered. Italy had a major presence in Libya with over 300,000 troops and some 300-plus aircraft against 36,000 Allied troops and fewer than 100 aircraft in the area. There were four

squadrons of Blenheims – Nos 45, 55, 113 and 211 – alongside the Army Co-operation Westland Lysanders and elderly Bristol Bombay troop transports that could be used as bombers if required. The RAF Blenheims based in Iraq and Aden were quite some distance away.

Furthermore, Italy was in a better location for supporting its Middle East operations and could call for reinforcements with ease from Sicily, but with the Mediterranean surrounded by the enemy, Britain could not easily protect its interests in the Middle East. The Army and RAF in that area would have to accept the burden of protecting those interests. Besides, there were no reinforcements – they were busy defending Britain.

Commanding 202 Group, later called the Desert Air Force, was a First World War ace with 60 confirmed victories – Air Commodore Raymond Collishaw. He was a man of action and immediately Italy declared war on Britain he sent six Blenheims on an armed reconnaissance mission over Libya. Collishaw wanted to know where the enemy was and what its strength was. Following the dawn flight on 11 June were eight fully armed Blenheims from 45 Squadron, which bombed the Italian airbase at El Adem outside Tobruk. This was a low-level surprise attack that clearly informed the Italians that they had a fight on their hands. The same afternoon, Collishaw sent 18 Blenheims from 55 and 113 Squadrons on another raid on El Adem. Both missions met with success and apart from serious damage to the airfield, not to mention Italian morale, some 20 enemy aircraft were destroyed or damaged. Three Blenheims from the first raid were lost and four others damaged in both raids. With such a small force of aircraft at his disposal, Collishaw believed that attacking the enemy first was the best defence. In this he was not wrong and it had the approval of his Air Officer Commanding, Air Chief Marshal Sir Arthur Longmore.

Collishaw did not let up and on 12 June a force of 28 Blenheims from 21, 45 and 55 Squadrons took off to bomb the harbour at Tobruk. Unfortunately, the weather was poor and only a few aircraft found and attacked Tobruk; other aircraft bombed targets that they spotted en route and four Blenheims landed back at base with their bombs still on board. While there were no RAF losses on the

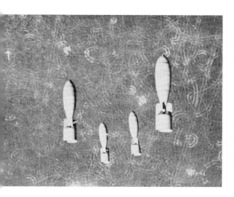

mission, three Blenheims were lost or damaged through accidents on the ground. Further missions against the Italians were mounted and in the first five days since 10 June Blenheims had flown 106 bombing sorties with varying success. Four aircraft were lost through enemy action and several were damaged, but they also shot down Italian fighters and bombed ships and troop positions as well as airstrips.

Collishaw used his few Blenheims wisely but not sparingly; the four Egyptian-based squadrons were used on a daily basis with raids on Italian army posts and airfields. There were three squadrons (45, 55 and 211) equipped with Mk Is and one (113) with the Blenheim Mk IV. As each day unfolded fewer aircraft were serviceable, but as long as there were Blenheims the attacks continued, even though ACM Longmore queried Collishaw's use of the Blenheim as a low-level strafing aircraft against defended targets. Nevertheless, he did promise reinforcements but these could not be ferried from Britain to Egypt as they would

ABOVE A series of three pictures showing four 250lb bombs from a 13 Squadron Blenheim being dropped over the desert. *(13 Squadron Archives)*

have to fly either over enemy-held territory or on a long arduous route which included a lengthy over-sea crossing. In the event Blenheims were crated, along with Hurricanes, and sent to Takoradi on the Gold Coast (now Ghana) to be reassembled and flown to Egypt. The first Blenheim arrived via this route in mid-September 1940.

Blenheims and other aircraft began to arrive on a regular basis and soon the older types, such as the Vickers Wellesley, had been replaced. This was fortuitous as the Italians, under Marshal Graziani, began to assemble in force to invade Egypt. They halted at Sidi Barrani on 16 September and dug in. Collishaw's photo-reconnaissance Blenheims had kept a regular watch on Graziani's movements and the information was of great value to General Wavell and the commanders of

LEFT Blenheim Mk IVs from 84 and 203 Squadrons seen flying outbound to attack Palmyra airfield during the first sortie by the RAF against Vichy French targets in Syria. *(Crown Copyright)*

the British and Commonwealth troops waiting for the battle. Blenheims also bombed and strafed the Italian positions and were later joined by Vickers Wellingtons to add to the bombing. On 9 December, General Richard O'Connor sent his armies in to attack Sidi Barrani; they captured their objective on 11 December and the Italians were chased out of Egypt.

Greek campaign

Although the Italians had been ousted from Egypt, the threat remained. However, because of the need to help Greece, many aircraft and troops were transferred to that theatre. While this was happening, General Erwin Rommel and the German Afrika Korps had arrived in North Africa to take over from the Italians; he wasted no time and on 24 March 1941, launched an attack which resulted in the fall of Benghazi in Libya on 3 April. The RAF was caught up in this rapidly changing scene and abandoned airfields as they lost ground. Blenheims of 45 and 55 Squadrons mounted several attacks on the German army and helped to stop their advance on Tobruk. Reinforcements, both on land and in the air, were urgently required if disaster was to be averted.

This was not easy – the route from Gibraltar through the Mediterranean was treacherous. Enemy submarines were on patrol and any shipping was within reach of Axis aircraft. Additionally, many of the RAF fighters and bombers had been sent to aid in the defence of Greece. Blenheims from 30, 84 and 211

Squadrons were in action during November 1940 bombing Italian targets in Albania. During these raids, which saw the Blenheim used as a fighter and a bomber, losses were sustained and two aircraft were lost to Italian fighters on 13 November, while another was shot down the next day. By the beginning of December the weather had deteriorated considerably; snow and ice added to the worsening visibility and adverse conditions made it difficult to keep aircraft serviceable. Nevertheless, sorties continued with regular attacks on Valona harbour in Albania and on Italian troop positions along the coast road between Albania and Greece.

Air Vice Marshal Arthur Tedder took over command from ACM Longmore and inherited an almost static air force. The winter rains continued and rendered the airfields muddy and waterlogged, making operations difficult. The sterling service by the groundcrews must be commended; they worked outdoors in all weathers so that aircraft would be ready for operations. Conditions were poor with all personnel living under canvas in a primitive environment. However, No 211 Squadron mounted several missions on the Albanian city of Elbasan in early January. They lost one Blenheim and others suffered damage, but the Italian positions were bombed despite enemy fighter activity.

The air war by the RAF to assist the Greeks in their fight against the Italians was fierce, but it has often been overlooked in histories of the war. Italy invaded Albania and was intent on using that country as a springboard to attack Greece, but they did not take into account the formidable fighting prowess of the Greek armed forces, which included 12 Blenheim Mk IVs purchased in 1939. They fought alongside the RAF aircraft and inflicted damage on the enemy, but as the battles continued and pushed the Italians back, the Germans took an interest. They had been building up forces in the Balkans and by spring 1941 were in a position to aid their Italian ally and attack the Greek positions in force. The RAF was, once again, in the midst of the action.

Germany invaded Greece from Bulgaria and moved quickly before the Greeks – who were heavily involved in fighting the Italians in southern Albania – could react. They could not fight on

BELOW Blenheim Mk I L6670 of 211 Squadron comes in to land at Menidi-Tatoi, Greece, in February 1941. *(Crown Copyright)*

both fronts and though assisted by their allies it was an uneven fight. RAF Blenheims were sent to bomb German troop positions in Yugoslavia and in the Strumica region with varied success. Reinforcements were required and Tedder sent Blenheims from Egypt to Crete to assist with the escalating battle. The German forces proved numerically superior and the Greeks continued to be pushed back, fighting valiantly all the way. On 13 April Blenheims of 211 Squadron carried out raids on troop positions with some success, but when they attempted a third mission later in the day they were intercepted by Messerschmitt Bf 109s and six of the seven Blenheims were shot down. Sadly, only two of the aircrew survived the action.

German aircraft, in turn, raided the bases from which the Blenheims were operating and several aircraft were destroyed or seriously damaged on the ground. As the Germans advanced into Greece the Allies withdrew and the RAF flew their remaining aircraft to airfields on Crete. To bolster the defence of the island, nine Blenheim IVFs from 203 Squadron were deployed from Aden. They were sorely needed as the enemy turned their attention to Crete. On 27 April the Germans took Athens and Greece was out of the war; the last of the Allied forces withdrew from Greece. Crete was not forgotten, though, and once the Germans had captured the airfields in southern Greece they could attack the island, which was important for control of that part of the Mediterranean. The Luftwaffe carried out intensive attacks on the Allied shipping convoys and on the airfields of

Crete. Defending the island were RAF fighters, including Blenheims, but they were seriously outnumbered. Aircraft losses mounted – some to mistaken fire from ships evacuating troops from the island – and the RAF was forced to withdraw. The remaining Blenheims from 11, 30, 84, 113, 203 and 211 Squadrons were flown to various bases in Egypt where they were all in need of repair.

Crete was invaded on 20 May by airborne paratroops who secured the airfields, allowing further German troops to land in the days that followed. The last of the Allied forces on the island were taken off from the south by the Royal Navy as the enemy was securing the north of the island.

This did not mark the end of the Blenheims and Crete; they operated from bases in Egypt to harass enemy shipping and even raid the airfields that they had so recently vacated. On 26 May four Blenheims from 45 Squadron were sent to bomb Maleme airfield. They were intercepted by Messerschmitt Bf 109s and two were shot down. Other raids on the airfield followed, but few aircraft managed to get to Malème and those that did caused little damage. By the end of May it was obvious that the Blenheims could not carry on, and so the raids were discontinued.

Having fought in the Greek campaign the Blenheims were back in action in the Desert War. Germany had come to the aid of their Italian ally and the RAF was busy attacking German positions. New Blenheims had been arriving via Takoradi and by long ferry flights

ABOVE Blenheim Mk IVs from 14 Squadron flying over the Western Desert in February 1942.
(Crown Copyright)

from the UK. The latter was a hazardous option and several aircraft were lost to enemy action.

On 30 July 1941, Collishaw handed over 204 Group to Air Vice Marshal Arthur Coningham. Collishaw had done a valiant job, but he was tired and needed a rest from operations. Coningham was a tough New Zealander who used the lull in the battle to get his force up to full strength. The Blenheims of 5, 11, 14, 55, 84, 113 and 203 Squadrons were joined by a detachment of 8 Squadron Blenheims and also by South African Air Force Blenheims from 15 Squadron. They were all fresh aircraft with rested crews who would now take part in Operation Crusader to relieve Tobruk. General Auchinleck launched the operation on 18 November 1941. Blenheim bombers and fighters attacked enemy supply columns and troop movements on a daily basis. Often the raids by Blenheims and other RAF bombers were made well beyond the front line, but at that stage the enemy fighter force was not up to strength and, although the RAF lost aircraft, they enjoyed considerable success. The Germans brought in reinforcements including the large, powerful and experienced Luftflotte II from the Eastern Front.

Operation Crusader captured Benghazi on 24 December and the battle continued as 1941 came to a close. The New Year saw the Desert War continue and the Blenheims were carrying out bombing and strafing missions on a regular basis. Interestingly, a few aircraft were converted locally to carry a 20mm Hispano cannon in the nose. This was mounted in the observer's position with the ammunition feed and box taking up the rest of the available space. It added firepower to the Blenheim and although the guns often jammed, they were effective in the strafing role.

Malta

Blenheims were also ferried from Britain to the island of Malta in the Mediterranean. Before the collapse of France the journey was across France and staged through Suez and on to Malta. With the fall of France the aircraft were fitted with a 100-gallon auxiliary fuel tank in the bomb bay for the flight from Cornwall to Gibraltar. Here they were refuelled and flown on to Malta. It was a dangerous but vital journey,

as the aircraft were required not only in Malta but also for operations in North Africa and the Western Desert.

No 21 Squadron was deployed to Malta in April 1941 to carry out bombing missions on enemy shipping taking supplies to the Afrika Korps. They met with some success and denied many a fuel tanker and supply ship that would have assisted the enemy forces. Soon 82 Squadron joined the Malta Blenheims and they also strafed and bombed enemy shipping. Keeping the aircraft serviceable were the dedicated groundcrews who worked under difficult conditions with scant cover, shortage of spares and very little rest. Their ceaseless work meant that the RAF continued the fight; in July 110 Squadron arrived and went straight into action. Their aircraft were joined by Blenheims of 105 Squadron, which was under the command of Wing Commander Hughie Edwards VC DFC (the first Blenheim pilot to be awarded the Victoria Cross). Blenheims took the fight to the enemy who were attacking the island with increasing ferocity. The RAF suffered serious casualties and lost numerous aircraft, many Blenheims among them. However, the AOC of RAF Malta, Air Vice Marshal Hugh Pughe Lloyd MC DFC, found an excellent method of replacing aircraft. When fighters and bombers staged through Malta on their way to the Middle East he retained many as replacements. The aircraft and crews were soon flying missions for RAF Malta.

The Battle for Malta was crucial for the Axis forces if they were to succeed in the desert campaign, and that this was denied was down to a small determined force of Royal Navy and RAF personnel who took the battle to the enemy. On the ground in Malta the Army kept up their anti-aircraft fire as well as carrying out a myriad of other duties. Above all, the people of Malta never for one moment lost heart or doubted their Allies on the island. In all the actions RAF Blenheims were on constant patrol and flying offensive sweeps to harass enemy shipping and troop movements. For example, on 11 August 1941, two sections of three 105 Squadron aircraft took off to raid a nitrate manufacturing plant in Crotone in southern Italy. The first flight missed the location and bombed some railway buildings, but the second section found and bombed the factory. Anti-aircraft fire from Italian ships moored offshore hit Squadron Leader George Goode's Blenheim as it came in to make a second run; the Blenheim crashed near Crotone and the crew were captured. A second aircraft was also hit and damaged but was able to get back to Luqa, Malta, where it crashed on landing.

It was 105 and 107 Squadrons that carried out most of the Blenheim sorties, spending long hours looking for enemy shipping en route to North Africa as well as strafing enemy positions in Libya. Other sorties included an attack on a factory and power station at Licata in Sicily on 30 August, when six aircraft from the two squadrons scored several hits. They made a return trip to the factory at Crotone on 1 September; seven aircraft flew in at low level to bomb the chemical works, the railway lines and ships in the harbour. All in all it was a successful raid, but the missions were taking their toll on aircraft and crews.

Blenheims continued their raids but, even though replacements were arriving on a regular basis, losses were mounting due to German fighter action. Renewed efforts by the Axis to conquer Malta meant that additional firepower was brought in. Germany increased its bombing raids on Malta and many aircraft were destroyed on the ground. As numbers decreased it was decided to move the remaining RAF bombers to safety and in March 1942 the few surviving Blenheims and Wellingtons were flown out of Malta to Egypt.

Enter the Mk V

By this stage many Blenheims were deployed to the Far East theatre, but those that remained in the Middle East continued operations against the Afrika Korps, where they were joined or replaced by the new Blenheim Mk V, or 'Bisley'. Unfortunately, this model was not ideal for desert conditions and serviceability became an issue, as did the high loss rate. It should have been clear that the aircraft design was now outdated, but with the lack of any modern replacement, it soldiered on. Apart from taking part in Operation Torch – the invasion of North Africa – the Mk V carried out several bombing missions against the enemy. For daylight raids fighters escorted the Blenheims, but later in the year when the weather deteriorated they

ABOVE An Italian ship under attack by Blenheim Mk IVs in the Mediterranean. *(Crown Copyright)*

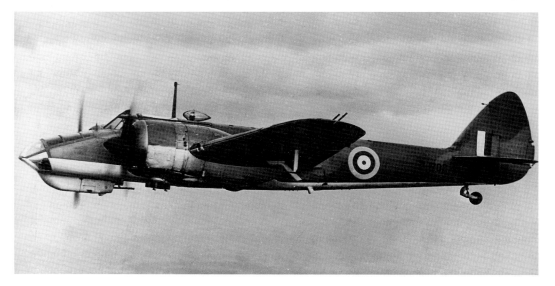

LEFT When it entered service, the Blenheim Mk V, or 'Bisley', unfortunately proved itself not ideal for desert conditions and serviceability became an issue. The aircraft's design was already outdated, but with the lack of any modern replacement it soldiered on in service. *(Crown Copyright)*

had to fly unescorted. One such sortie was on 4 December 1942 when Wing Commander Hugh Malcolm led 11 Blenheims to attack a Luftwaffe landing ground in Tunisia. One aircraft crashed on take-off and another had engine trouble and crash-landed, but the remaining nine continued. They were intercepted by Messerschmitt Bf 109s and shot down, and although his Blenheim had been hit, Malcolm pressed on to the target. He was later chased and brought down. He was awarded the Victoria Cross posthumously – the second Blenheim pilot to receive the VC.

Blenheims became restricted to night operations and as more modern types arrived in theatre the aircraft was relegated to maritime duties. By the end of 1943 they had been replaced by Lockheed Venturas. Just one squadron, No 614, continued to use the Mk V on maritime patrols in the Mediterranean until January 1944, when it was disbanded. Production of the Mk V had ceased in June 1943 and the Blenheim was out of front-line service in the Middle East. Already outdated by the time it went into battle, the Blenheim had served with distinction in the Mediterranean and Middle East theatres, but it continued in the Far East theatre for some months to come.

South-East Asia

Blenheim Is had been based in South-East Asia since August 1939, when 39 Squadron had moved from India to Tengah in Singapore. In September that year the unit was joined by 62 Squadron, also equipped with Blenheims. By the time Japanese forces attacked Malaya in early December 1941, 34 and 60 Squadrons were based at Tengah, No 39 having moved to the Middle East. No 34 Squadron was flying Blenheim Mk IVs, though No 62 was still equipped with Mk Is. No 62 Squadron was based on the Malayan mainland at Alor Star. However, as soon as the Japanese invasion began, the unit moved to Butterworth.

Once again facing more modern and capable fighters, the Blenheims suffered heavy losses. This led to the aircraft being forced back, moving to bases on Sumatra and Java where they were joined by 84 and 211 Squadrons with Blenheim IVs, which had been sent from Egypt to reinforce the area. Owing to being outclassed and heavily outnumbered, the personnel of all the squadrons in theatre were evacuated to India.

Blenheim squadrons participated in the drawn-out campaign in Burma, with 11, 34, 45, 60 and 84 Squadrons flying frequent

RIGHT Blenheim Mk Is of 62 Squadron have their engines fired up at an aerodrome in Singapore during 1941.
(Crown Copyright)

attacks on the Japanese forces advancing north through the jungle. They also flew raids on enemy bases in the south of the country. However, unable to efficiently perform against fighters such as the Mitsubishi A6M Zero, the Blenheims were replaced by Hurricane IIC fighter-bombers, which were faster and better equipped to defend themselves against the enemy fighters.

Despite the odds stacked against them, the Blenheim crews had once again made a significant difference and had even notched up some notable achievements in this theatre. Squadron Leader Arthur Scarf was posthumously awarded the Victoria Cross for an attack on Singora, Thailand, on 9 December 1941, becoming the third Blenheim pilot to be awarded Britain's highest gallantry award. Furthermore, a Blenheim of 60 Squadron RAF was credited with shooting down Lieutenant Colonel Tateo Katō's Nakajima Ki-43 fighter and badly damaging two others in a single engagement over the Bay of Bengal on 22 May 1942. Katō attacked the flight of Blenheims and, as he pulled up after making his first diving pass, turret gunner Flight Sergeant 'Jock' McLuckie raked the fighter's underside with

a long burst and the Ki-43 started to burn and crashed into the sea. Katō's death was a severe blow to the Imperial Japanese Army Air Force and a great morale boost to the Blenheim crews.

The last RAF Blenheims flown in action were the Mk IVs of 60 Squadron, based at Yelahanaka in India. This unit was re-equipped with Hurricane Mk IICs in August 1943 and so the Blenheim's operational front-line service with the RAF came to a close.

ABOVE A picture taken during a low-level attack by Blenheims from 60 Squadron, which are levelling out for the run-in to make a masthead-height attack on a Japanese coaster off Akyab, Burma, on 10 November 1942. *(Crown Copyright)*

LEFT Groundcrew unload medical equipment from Blenheim Mk V BA576/N of 34 Squadron at an airfield in India *c*1943. *(Crown Copyright)*

Chapter Two

Restore to flight

Since the end of the Second World War there have only been three completed private restorations of a Blenheim to flight, making it one of the world's rarest warbirds. Each of these major restoration projects have involved countless hours of time, skill, specialist knowledge, patience, access to the necessary components and considerable amounts of money.

'The project not only resulted in the restoration of a unique historical aircraft, but also brought to the public's attention the heroic actions of Blenheim aircrews during the difficult early years of World War Two.'

Raymond Baxter,
former RAF pilot and TV presenter

OPPOSITE Blenheim Mk I L6739 in ARC's workshops at Duxford in August 2014, while work was being carried out on the port engine, which had developed an oil leak during an early ground run. Setbacks such as this during any warbird restoration highlight how important patience is among the many requirements necessary to complete a complicated project where absolutely nothing can be left to chance. *(Jarrod Cotter)*

RIGHT Although many of the Canadian Bolingbrokes sold as surplus were in undamaged ex-service condition, others had suffered accidents such as this example, which highlights the restorer's many challenges when beginning a project from scratch. *(RCAF)*

BELOW The ARC storage facility has many spare parts from Bolingbrokes, including a rack full of engines. *(Jarrod Cotter)*

These major restorations have taken numerous years to complete, and being such a rare aircraft it is fortunate that some of the same key personnel have been part of the teams on each occasion. In this chapter we go behind the scenes of the Aircraft Restoration Company to get some idea of the very challenging work involved to get the world's only airworthy example of its type back in the air.

No complete examples of a Blenheim survived in Britain after the war. There were, however, numerous survivors in Canada in the form of the Bristol Bolingbroke (licence-built Blenheims used by the Royal Canadian Air Force) and also licence-built aircraft in Finland. Following their withdrawal in Canada, however, none were kept airworthy (though the type did continue flying in Finland until 1958).

Many surplus wartime aircraft were bought by Canadian farmers, who used a number of the components from them for various purposes around their farms and drained them of any valuable oil and fuel which was left in their tanks. During the 1970s pioneer preservationist Ormond Haydon-Baillie bought two Bolingbrokes – 9893 and 10038 – plus numerous more engines and propellers, and had them shipped to the Imperial War Museum at Duxford in Cambridgeshire. The Blenheims

BELOW ARC also has a spare Bolingbroke centre section in storage. *(Jarrod Cotter)*

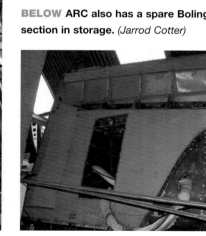

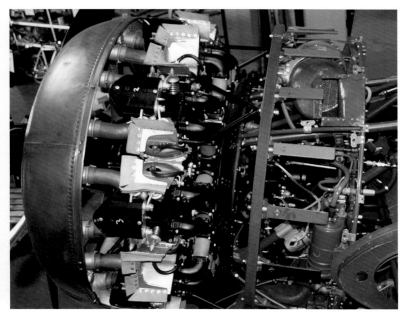

were initially stored in one of Duxford's hangars, but their owner negotiated with the IWM to try to secure a workshop in which to restore them. He succeeded and was given Building 66. Part of Ormond Haydon-Baillie's early team of volunteers included John Romain, who for many years now has been a historic aircraft restoration specialist as well as one of the world's most experienced warbird pilots.

Tragically Ormond Haydon-Baillie was killed in a crash in July 1977, and his collection was sold off. It was Graham Warner, who sadly

died before L6739 took flight, who bought the Blenheims. Graham offered John Romain the restoration of the Blenheim project, as he had recently completed an apprenticeship with British Aerospace. He then sat exams to obtain the necessary CAA licences required to carry out a restoration to flight of an aircraft such as this.

The fuselage used was 10038, for which the appropriate civilian registration G-MKIV was chosen. It first flew on 22 May 1987, piloted by John Larcombe with John Romain (seated in what became the engineer's seat in a

ABOVE Before and after photos showing the condition of an 'as found' Bristol Mercury engine, and a meticulously restored example. *(Jarrod Cotter)*

FAR LEFT AND LEFT Another pair of comparison photos, this time highlighting the difference between an unrestored and a restored cylinder head unit. *(Jarrod Cotter)*

restored Blenheim). The Blenheim was painted as V6028/GB-D of 105 Squadron, as flown by Wing Commander 'Hughie' Edwards VC. It flew to great acclaim at several events, much to the particular delight of all the 'Blenheim Boys'.

However, on 21 June 1987, just a month after its maiden flight, G-MKIV crashed at Denham following an unscheduled touch-and-go by the aircraft's reserve pilot. Also on board were John Romain and John 'Smudge' Smith, and thankfully all three survived. The Blenheim was a write-off, but Graham Warner organised a press call just a few days later and announced that another example of the type would be rebuilt to fly. John and Graham then formed the Aircraft Restoration Company.

Bolingbroke 10201 of the Strathallan

Collection in Scotland was chosen as the basis for the second restoration project, and using all the team's experience gained from G-MKIV this aircraft was flying after five years of work in an all-over black paint scheme as Z5722/WM-Z of 68 Squadron, and registered as G-BPIV. Its first post-restoration flight took place on 18 May 1993, when it was piloted by Hoof Proudfoot with John Romain again in the right-hand seat.

Over the next ten years the aircraft was a hugely popular sight at air shows, especially as – apart from Avro Lancaster Mk I PA474 of the RAF's Battle of Britain Memorial Flight – it was the only other airworthy Second World War-era British bomber in the UK, and the only flying example of an early war RAF light bomber.

Sadly, while returning to Duxford from an event in 2003, G-BPIV suffered a landing accident at its home airfield. The historic aviation community was devastated, especially all those involved very closely with the project.

Not to be beaten

The feeling of loss among all those who had spent countless hours restoring and then caring meticulously for G-BPIV for ten years can be easily understood, and initially there was much consideration given as to how to proceed. Graham Warner later transferred the airframe to John Romain and, undefeated by a second accident beyond his control, John then formed a new company called Blenheim Duxford Ltd, under the umbrella of which a new restoration project would begin.

There was to be a significant twist in the story, though. After the war, Bristol employee Ralph Nelson bought a Blenheim Mk I nose section, and he later converted it into an electric car. During the nose's transformation into a car Ralph retained all the equipment he removed from it and also any metalwork that was cut away for its transformation. Realising its importance, Ralph donated the car to the Duxford Blenheim project, and when faced with another rebuild some years later the team decided that to distance the project from their previous work they would restore the Mk I nose for the Blenheim. As John 'Smudge' Smith described it to the author at the time: 'This way

it will be like restoring a completely different aircraft, and not doing it all over again.'

The nose was from Avro-built Mk IF L6739/YP-Q, which was on the strength of 23 Squadron based at Collyweston in Northamptonshire from September 1939. This aircraft flew on night-fighter sorties during the Battle of Britain, so it came with greatly important provenance.

However, by choosing to do this the team gave themselves a huge amount more work, estimated to be in the region of an extra two years plus. But the end result, as illustrated in this book, has already been – and will be much more so – appreciated by a massive audience as it embarks on its first display season at around the same time this book is released in 2015. Very few people alive will have ever seen a Blenheim Mk I fly, and the aircraft was already getting lots of enquiries for air show bookings for events in 2015 as soon as it had first flown in November 2014.

As G-BPIV had been such a popular performer in its former Mk IV guise, post-accident reporting was colossal as the nation's interest in the future of this much-loved aircraft grew. Therefore the latest restoration has been recorded in great detail, as veterans and enthusiasts were longing for regular updates of its progress. This makes L6739 an ideal candidate for this Haynes Owners' Workshop Manual, as not only is it the world's only airworthy Blenheim and the only complete Blenheim Mk I, but every major step of its complex restoration was available to be seen.

Approval basis

For this restoration, in the Civilian Aviation Authority (CAA) Airworthiness Approval Note (AAN) the aircraft was designated as a Bolingbroke Mk I conversion. It was based on the previous Fairchild Bolingbroke IV-T project which was approved under AAN No 21124 dated 28 May 1987, but was to be installed with an original Blenheim Mk I nose and to retain Bristol Mercury XX engines and de Havilland propellers, which had been part of the first approval. Because the Mk I nose was to become part of the restoration, a new issue of AAN 21124 needed to be raised, which was issue 3.

The Blenheim is classified as a 'Simple' type within the definition of British Civil Airworthiness Requirements (BCAR) A8-20 Para 1.2.1(a).

were made. Any such work was carried out in accordance with the manufacturer's repair manual, and some lower skins and formers required attention.

Restoration of the Mk I nose initially began in ARC's smaller workshop on the main IWM Duxford site, immediately north of the famous 'Hangar Base' area, which was the hangar seen destroyed in the iconic film *Battle of Britain*. It was subject to an in-depth restoration by ARC and specialist contractors in the UK defined by ARC's CAA Approval No DAI/9459/94.

Both engine mount assemblies, including the mounting bolts, were NDT inspected and found to be all satisfactory. Some sections of the firewall needed to be replaced, and the new alternate material complied with the necessary approval. The final product was inspected by ARC and found to be in satisfactory airworthy condition.

The wings had any necessary structural repairs, alterations or replacements carried out in accordance with the original manufacturer's repair drawings and AP1530 using material and fasteners conforming to the original specification, gauge, form and configuration unless otherwise defined. The repaired areas were limited to leading edge skins and structure at the inboard end, lower wing tank access panels and undercarriage nacelles. These, along with the tailplanes, were

Approval of the aircraft for the issue of a Permit to Fly was based on an investigation of the modification state and build standard in accordance with BCAR A3-7. Any new modifications were assessed against the requirements of BCAR section K as appropriate.

Blenheim rebirth

The rear fuselage, which had been in place during the 2003 landing accident, was thoroughly inspected and any necessary repairs

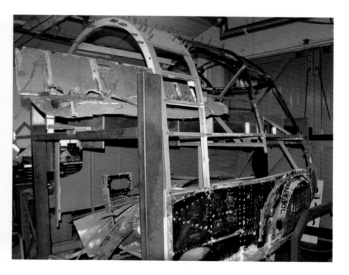

(All photos this page François Prins)

ABOVE LEFT Blenheim Mk I L6739's nose at the beginning of its restoration back from a car into part of an aircraft. Note that the front wheel arch area is still evident!

ABOVE Another view of the Blenheim's nose, with new material visible riveted into position at the top rear area.

LEFT With much of its refurbished skin panelling in place, the Mk I nose awaits glazing.

RIGHT Work begins on fitting out the interior of the Mk I cockpit, with the engine control levers visible in place on the left side.

BELOW A wide-angle view of the Mk I nose interior in the very early stages of being fitted out.

ABOVE While the nose was making progress in ARC's workshop on Duxford's main site, inside Hangar 3 great strides were being made in the restoration of the fuselage, wings and undercarriage. *(François Prins)*

LEFT Once work on the Mk I nose was at an appropriate stage, it was fitted to the fuselage of G-BPIV, proving that the Blenheim's design has a common joint at this point. *(François Prins)*

BELOW LEFT Headway is being made to the engine nacelles and undercarriage units. *(François Prins)*

BELOW Inside the cockpit the trim and flying controls are seen uncovered to reveal the progress that was being made to them out of sight inside the historic machine. *(Jarrod Cotter)*

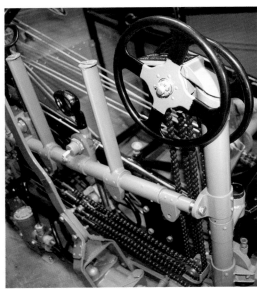

RIGHT While reconstruction of the fuselage was underway in Hangar 3, a dedicated team began to assemble the restored components of the Mercury engines in the ARC workshops. (Jarrod Cotter)

then inspected by ARC and found to be in satisfactory airworthy condition.

All flying control surfaces – rudder, ailerons, elevators and the wing flaps – were inspected and also found to be in airworthy condition. They were then refitted on to the aircraft in accordance with AP1530. The flying control system was also dismantled, cleaned and inspected. All components, assemblies and pulleys were repaired, overhauled or replaced as required. New flying control cables were then installed, rigged and tensioned in accordance with the maintenance manual.

Engines and propellers

G-BPIV is fitted with two Bristol Mercury XX nine-cylinder single-stage supercharged radial engines. These, along with a third engine to act as a spare, were meticulously overhauled by ARC in accordance with AP1491D. The engines' serial numbers are S51023 to port and S56884 to starboard.

The Blenheim is fitted with two de Havilland 4/3 three-bladed bracket-type two-pitch non-feathering propellers. These are of 10ft 9in diameter with de Havilland blade type P55409/B. The fine and coarse pitch settings are 26° and 34° 45' respectively. The hub and blade combination is one of the permitted combinations for the Blenheim and was

CENTRE After many hours of concentrated work the Blenheim's port engine comes together, seen here in August 2012. (Jarrod Cotter)

RIGHT With the restoration of the aircraft's Mercury engines gathering pace, the Blenheim was moved from Duxford's Hangar 3 into the ARC workshops where it is seen in November 2012. As by this stage the identity of the aircraft from which the nose came from had been discovered, note that on the side there is a paint diagram showing what camouflage would be applied. (Jarrod Cotter)

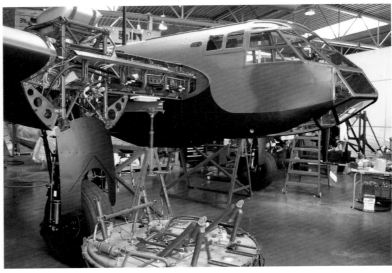

ABOVE LEFT The starboard Mercury engine nears completion in November 2012 as the cylinder heads are placed in front of it prior to being refitted. *(Jarrod Cotter)*

ABOVE Seen during August 2013, the Blenheim has been painted into an early war night-fighter camouflage scheme. The starboard engine mount is yet to be fitted at this stage. *(Jarrod Cotter)*

LEFT The port engine mount in place in August 2014, awaiting the restored Bristol Mercury XX. *(Jarrod Cotter)*

BELOW LEFT The port Bristol Mercury with one piston and cylinder head not yet refitted. *(Jarrod Cotter)*

BELOW A cylinder head and piston from the port engine undergoing remedial work. *(Jarrod Cotter)*

approved under AAN 21125 issue 1.

Fuel and oil

The basic fuel system was installed and two original serviceable fuel tanks were refurbished and pressure tested to 1.5psi. The fuel system hoses were replaced with modern MIL-DTL-6000 specification hoses.

The oil system was dismantled, cleaned and inspected in accordance with the maintenance instructions contained in AP1530. All the components, parts, tanks, filters, coolers and pipework were repaired, overhauled or replaced and functionally tested in accordance with the relevant service instruction or maintenance manual. Oil system hoses were also replaced with those to the MIL-DTL-6000 specification.

Hydraulics and pneumatics

The hydraulic system was dismantled, cleaned and inspected in accordance with AP1530. All components, valves, selectors and actuators were repaired, overhauled or replaced and functionally tested. All system rigid pipe lines were replaced with Tungum alloy tube to specification DTD5019, and all flexible lines with Aeroquip 303 conforming to specification MIL-DTL-8794E.

The pneumatic system was completely dismantled, cleaned and inspected in accordance with AP1530A. Again all the components,

valves, selectors and actuators were repaired, overhauled or replaced and functionally tested. The pneumatic bottle was inspected and subject to a hydrostatic test by ARC.

The pneumatic system is charged from an engine-driven BTH-type AV compressor. All system rigid pipe lines were replaced with Tungum alloy tube to specification DTD5019, and all flexible lines with Aeroquip 303 conforming to specification MIL-DTL-8794E. Both systems were then reassembled and fitted into the aircraft.

Electrical system

The Blenheim's electrical system was rewired in accordance with AP1530 and all electrical plugs and sockets were replaced

ABOVE Modern radio and transponder equipment has been fitted to the lower part of the pilot's main instrument panel, seen in place here (lower right). *(Jarrod Cotter)*

Mode 'S' transponder suite have been installed into the pilot's lower instrument panel. The units installed are a Becker RT6201 VHF radio and a Becker BXP6402-1-(01) transponder.

Mk I changes

All marks of Blenheim incorporated a standard production break on the main fuselage for the attachment of the aircraft's nose. Therefore all was in place for the rebuilt Mk I nose to be fitted – however, there were major changes with regards to the location of the controls.

Whereas the Mk IV had the engine controls in the centre of the cockpit, on the Mk I they are on the left – throttle, mixture and push-pull controls are all on that side. Changes to the fuel system for a Blenheim I involve only the location and method of operation of the fuel valve and selector within the cockpit. Mk I selectors are installed on the right-hand side wall and operate the fuel valves by means of a Teleflex cable system to the valve mounted on the rear of the engine firewall. Fuel gauges are located on the left-hand side of the cockpit adjacent to the pilot.

Changes to the hydraulic system for a Blenheim I were also only the location and method of operation of the selector in the cockpit. This variant's selectors are installed in a central console and operated by stirrup handles, and a safety catch is installed on the undercarriage selector to prevent inadvertent operation.

Of note is that an authentic Mk IF gun pack has been fitted to the Blenheim. This is a large externally mounted unit positioned on the lower central fuselage and contains four replica 0.303in Browning machine guns.

After ten years of work, on Monday 12 August 2014, a milestone was reached when the Blenheim was rolled out for the first time wearing its new Mk I paint scheme. The history of the aeroplane's distinctive Mk I short nose has been thoroughly researched and traced back to Blenheim Mk I L6739, which, as already mentioned, served as a night-fighter with 23 Squadron, and thus the Bolingbroke fuselage was given the YP-Q code which that aircraft was allocated during its wartime service.

with new parts conforming to the original specification. The aircraft was rewired with modern electrical Raychem Type 44 cable to specification M22759 (dual wall construction). All switches, fuse boxes, generator controls and instrumentation were cleaned, inspected and replaced with new or overhauled components as required.

A Jasco Alternator was installed in place of the original generator to improve the electrical system. A modification was raised to detail the changes made for this alteration.

Radio/avionics

The original period military radio equipment was removed. Instead, a modern civil communications radio and air traffic VHF

ABOVE The Blenheim's original builder's plate has been fitted back inside the nose section, highlighting that it is a Mk I constructed by Avro in Manchester. *(Jarrod Cotter)*

RIGHT The short-nose Blenheim Mk I profile is evident in this view of L6739 nearing the completion of its restoration in ARC's Building 425 complex during September 2014. *(Jarrod Cotter)*

BELOW The finished result. Following an early air test on 3 December 2014, L6739 heads home for Duxford, flown by John Romain. *(Jarrod Cotter)*

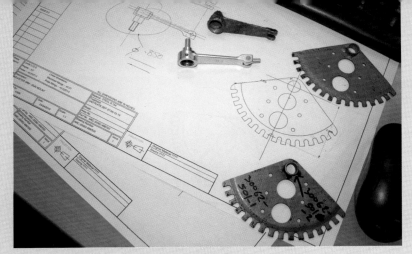

REPAIR, RECONDITION OR REVERSE ENGINEER?

In late 2011 Hawker Hurricane Mk IIc PZ865 flew to Duxford to begin its major maintenance with ARC. This was to include the refurbishment of the complete fuselage assembly. With the Hurricane's complex construction, this presented many intricate technical problems, the solution to just one of which is highlighted here to show how far advanced ARC's facilities have become these days, enabling work to be done that wasn't possible even just a few years ago. Some components for the Blenheim were remanufactured by using exactly the same process as described here.

The structural part of the Hurricane fuselage comprises a Warren truss framework. The main members are fabricated from either steel or Duralumin tube. The majority of the top, bottom and cross structures are braced with tie-rods and streamline wires, while the side structures are braced with tubes.

No welding is used to join the structure, as it is held together with mechanically fastened joints. Tubes are either rolled to a square section at joints, or have suitable plug ends fitted, and are then joined with plates or cluster joints.

As the framework contains several 'structurally significant items', the maintenance policy for the structure comprises general visual examinations during each annual winter maintenance and subsequent maintenance packages, plus an X-ray every 18 years (every third Major). Based on the findings during ARC's initial survey of PZ865, it was recommended that the fuselage should be dismantled for inspection in lieu of the pending X-ray. That was agreed by the project team, and the decision was vindicated by the

discovery of several significant faults including corrosion and cracking.

The component concentrated on here is a port cluster joint. In all there are four cluster joints, which attach the fuselage to the wing centre section. These are quite complex joints, which comprise some 132 individual components including eight structural members and three structurally significant items. Failure of one of these joints could be very serious indeed.

After the fuselage had been dismantled all the components were processed. This included establishing the provenance of the part, an initial visual examination, then a paint strip and cleaning which was followed by a further visual examination. Any faults were noted and rectified before the components were refinished, including NDT (non-destructive testing) for items that were critical to the airworthiness of the aircraft.

The cluster joint in question was an original item from 1944, which had the original inspector's stamp on it. It passed through the inspection process, including cadmium plating, all the way to the final NDT examination when it was declared unserviceable. The magnetic particle inspection discovered numerous fine cracks on the item, some of which were through the full material thickness. Further examination of the cracks revealed that some were in line and in close proximity to each other, though none had joined together. They were randomly placed along wherever the greatest forming of the material had taken place and were not emanating from any of the likely points of in-service stress concentrations.

The item was machined from a forging, so it was decided that the cracks had originated during the initial mass-manufacturing process, possibly through the metal not being hot and ductile enough during the forging process. They were not considered attributable to deterioration in service and so there was no probable risk to other airworthy Hurricanes.

However, a new identical part needed to be remanufactured. These items were originally machined from forgings, but that would be too expensive for a single replacement part, so it would instead be machined from billet. The original material specification was no longer

available, and that, coupled with different manufacturing processes, would require the use of an alternative material.

ARC had the original drawings, but as these were for a forged item they only provided detail for the final finish machining. Therefore a new set of drawings was required to machine the component from billet. These were produced from first principles by an in-house draughtsman.

The CAD (computer-assisted design) drawings provided all the information for ARC machinists to produce the joint. There were ten drawings altogether, showing all the views and sections the machinists needed. The drawing set also facilitated an engineering report that was required to substantiate both the change of material to a currently available specification, and also the change of manufacturing process.

The material recommended in the engineering report was S.98 steel, as that is sufficiently strong and also has the necessary resistance to fatigue. However, the billet size required was of 8in diameter, and that is only available in S.99, so the billet would require heat treatment to anneal it down to S.98 specification. But there was a complication with this, as owing to the thickness of the metal it would not be possible to obtain the correct heat treatment all the way through. This problem was overcome by boring out the centre of two billets prior to the heat treatment, allowing one to act as a test piece. It took three attempts to get a billet within the correct S.98 specification.

The billet was next sized internally and externally on a CNC lathe. Two 'flats' were then machined on the company's four-axis CNC milling machine to enable fixing, while the required six groups of machining operations were carried out to produce the new component. Prior to the sixth group of

machining operations, the joint was trial fitted to check the alignment of all holes and to ream any necessary to the final size required.

The new cluster joint took 80 hours of planning, setting, programming and machining to create. Once fully machined it went to the inspection department for a 100% dimension check. It was then sent off for cadmium plating, from which it emerged with a gold colour that was the result of the added chromates to enhance the item's corrosion-protective qualities.

The final stage of the process was for it to undergo NDT. During this the joint was placed in a magnetic field which any cracks present would disrupt and the minute magnetic particles would collect in a spray at the crack and provide an indication under ultraviolet light. Having passed the NDT, the inspection process was completed by checking the thickness of the cadmium plating and adding the relevant part number. The new joint was then painted and fitted to the Hurricane's fuselage. Altogether some 279 items were remanufactured for PZ865's Major maintenance, highlighting how 'reverse engineering' using state-of-the-art processes can keep historic aircraft in the air through the manufacture of long-obsolete and complicated-to-manufacture components.

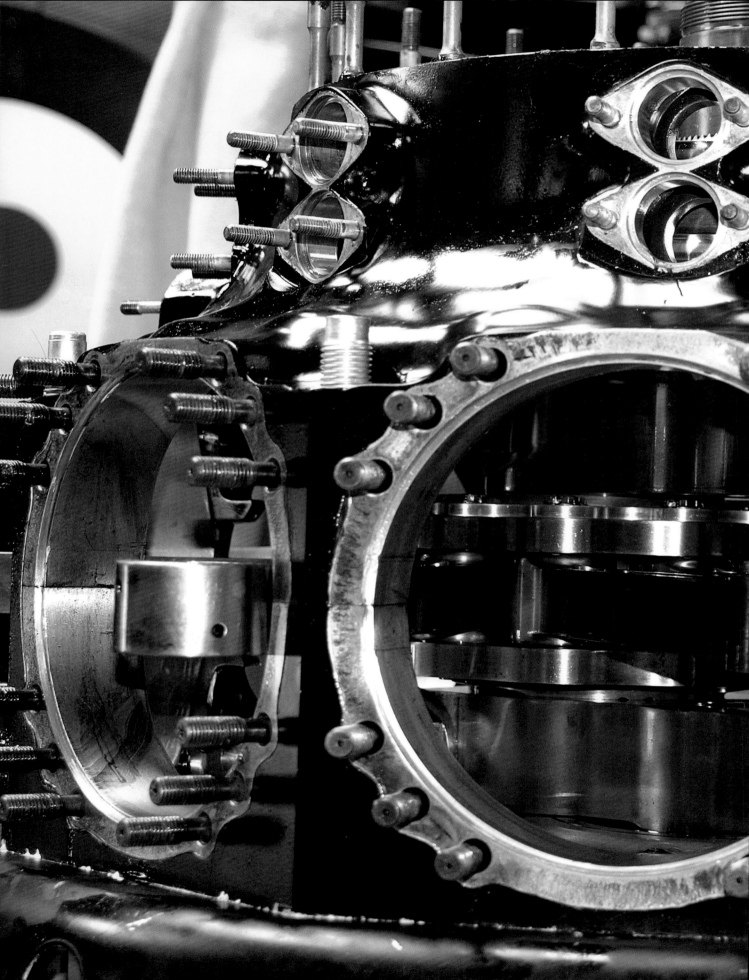

'This machine is a direct development of the Bristol Type 142 twin-engined high-speed transport monoplane.'

Frank Barnwell, in a covering letter submitted with the general layout drawings of the Type 142M to the Air Ministry for a design conference on 9 July 1935

Chapter Three

Anatomy of the Blenheim

When first flown in 1935 the Blenheim was a revolution in both design and performance to the pre-war RAF pilots who were familiar with biplanes. In this section we look at the structure of this ground-breaking aircraft by examining areas such as its airframe, engine, undercarriage, systems and armament. There is also a detailed look inside L6739, the world's only airworthy Blenheim and the only complete Mk I.

OPPOSITE The internal workings of a Bristol Mercury XX are revealed in this close-up of a partly disassembled engine. (*Jarrod Cotter*)

Bristol Blenheim Mk I cutaway. *(Mike Badrocke)*

1 Starboard navigation light
2 Starboard formation light
3 Wing rib construction
4 Aileron control rod
5 Starboard aileron
6 Aileron tab
7 Starboard outer flap
8 Outer wing panel torsion box
9 Wing leading edge (contains aileron control rods)
10 Starboard nacelle fairing
11 Starboard fuel tank, capacity 140 Imp gal
12 Oil tank, capacity 11½ Imp gal
13 Engine bearers
14 Oil cooler exhaust duct
15 Engine cooling air flaps
16 Cowling blister fairings
17 Bristol Mercury VIII nine-cylinder air-cooled radial engine
18 Oil coiler ram air intakes
19 Propeller hub mechanism
20 de Havilland three-bladed variable-pitch propeller
21 Carburettor air intake
22 Cabin air intake
23 Nose compartment glazing
24 Drift sight
25 Pitot tubes
26 Rudder pedals
27 Bomb-aimer's folding seat
28 Pilot's instrument panel
29 Direct vision side window panel
30 Control column
31 Instrument venture tube
32 Seat adjustment lever
33 Engine throttle levers
34 Pilot's seat
35 Navigator/bomb-aimer's seat
36 Fuel cocks
37 Parachute stowage
38 Cockpit roof sliding hatch
39 Engine instruments
40 Sliding hatch rails
41 Wing centre section construction
42 Aerial mast
43 Parachute stowage
44 Wing/fuselage attachment main frame
45 Pneumatic system compressed air bottle
46 Three-man dinghy
47 First-aid box
48 Fuselage double frame
49 Rear gunner's entry/ emergency escape hatch
50 Rear gunner's seat
51 Gun turret
52 Ammunition belt feed
53 Browning 0.303in machine gun
54 Aerial cable lead-in
55 Fuselage skin plating
56 Starboard tailplane
57 Starboard elevator
58 HF aerial cable
59 Fin construction
60 Rudder mass balance
61 Fabric-covered rudder construction
62 Sternpost
63 Rudder trim tab
64 Tail navigation light
65 Elevator trim tab
66 Fabric-covered elevator construction
67 Elevator balance
68 Port tailplane
69 Rudder cables
70 Elevator hinge control
71 Tailwheel shock absorber
72 Tailwheel
73 Control cable cross-shaft
74 Tail assembly joint rig
75 Rear fuselage frames
76 Fuselage stringer construction
77 Control cables
78 Access steps
79 Light Series bomb racks, port and starboard
80 Two 4FL flares
81 Trailing edge flap shroud
82 Flap jack
83 Inboard split trailing edge flap
84 Outer wing spar attachment joint
85 Flap lever mechanism
86 Outboard split trailing edge flap
87 Rear spar
88 Aileron hinge control

89 Aileron trim tab
90 Fabric-covered aileron construction
91 Port formation flight
92 Wingtip construction
93 Port navigation light
94 Landing/taxiing lamps
95 Wing rib construction
96 Front spar
97 Aileron control rod
98 Leading edge nose ribs
99 Ammunition tank
100 Fixed Browning 0.303in machine gun
101 Outer wing panel torsion box
102 Centre section/outer wing joint
103 Mainwheel well
104 Centre section main spar

105 Main oil tank, capacity 11½ Imp gal
106 Nacelle fairing
107 Port fuel tank, capacity 140 Imp gal
108 Control cable runs
109 Oil cooler
110 Engine cooling air flaps
111 Main undercarriage retraction jack
112 Mainwheel shock absorber leg struts
113 Rear breaker strut
114 Port mainwheel
115 Leg fairing door

116 Carburettor air intake
117 Engine bearer
118 Exhaust collector ring
119 Oil cooler ram air intakes
120 Propeller hub pitch-change mechanism
121 de Havilland three-bladed variable-pitch propeller
122 Two-cell bomb bay
123 Bomb carriers
124 250lb high-explosive bombs
125 Bomb-bay doors

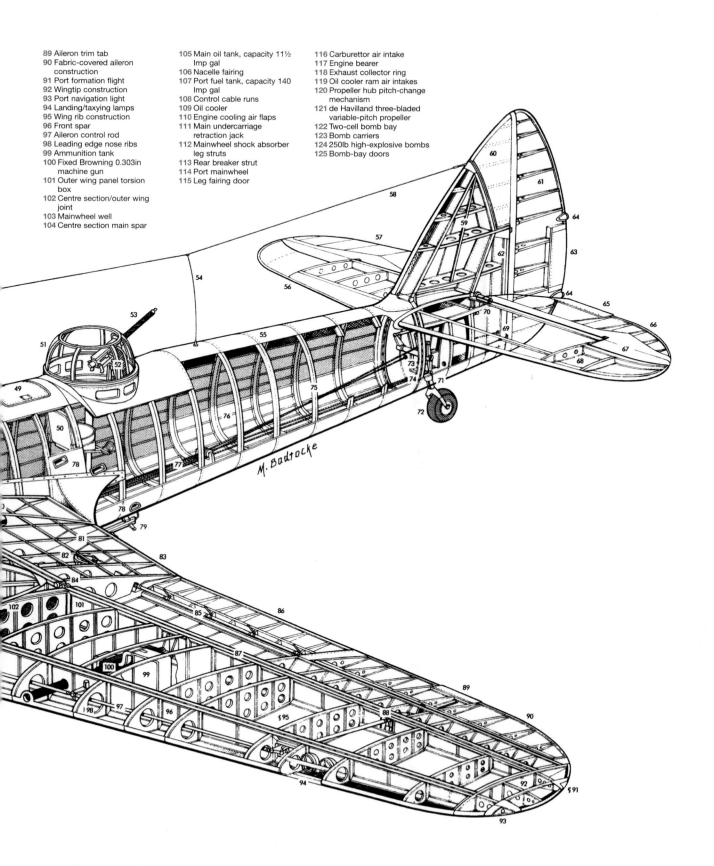

M. Badrocke

The Bristol Blenheim is an all-metal low-wing monoplane, powered by two Bristol Mercury engines fitted with variable-pitch propellers. It was designed and equipped for day-bombing and its crew comprised three members: pilot, bomb-aimer or navigator and gunner or wireless operator.

Fuselage

The Blenheim's fuselage is of all-metal monocoque construction throughout, with alclad (a corrosion-resistant aluminium sheet formed from high-purity aluminium surface layers metallurgically bonded to high-strength aluminium alloy core material) being used for the skin, stringers and formers. It is constructed by the joining of three sections – the front fuselage (pilot's cockpit), the rear fuselage (the main cabin portion) and the stern frame. Members, formers and bulkheads are designated according to their distance in inches from former '0', from the aft face of the rearmost member of the front fuselage.

The fuselage front and rear portions are directly connected at their upper peripheries by means of the front fuselage skin overlap, while the centre mainplane provides means of rigid attachment at the fuselage front and rear lower portions, a substantial central keel extending between the aft transverse member (at former 12in) of the front fuselage and bulkhead (81in) of the rear fuselage. The fuselage stern frame is secured to the rear fuselage by means of its skin forward overlap along the whole of its periphery. The skin covering throughout the fuselage is secured to the fuselage formers by means of ³⁄₃₂in-diameter snap-head Duralumin rivets, except at the end formers, where the rivets are countersunk and flush. The covering sheeting is lap-jointed – upper and forward sheets overlapping lower and aft sheets respectively – with the vertical overlapping external edges being faired.

The front fuselage, in which is situated the pilot's cockpit, houses the pilot's control chassis and the flying and engine controls. In the roof of the rear fuselage is mounted the

BELOW **Blenheim I L6739 basks in some glorious sunshine outside ARC's hangar on 3 December 2014, where the angle of the light clearly shows the panelling and riveting of the all-metal fuselage.** *(Jarrod Cotter)*

gun turret, the wireless operator's station being immediately aft of this gun station. The fuselage stern frame, integral with the tail unit, houses the tailwheel compression strut, the rudder control aft levers and the counter shaft.

Mk IV front fuselage

This portion is constructed of light-alloy longitudinals and formers, the skin being alclad, while the windscreen framework is of light-alloy tube. Access to or exit from the cockpit is gained through the roof, which is covered by a transversely rounded sliding transparent hood or panel, the longitudinal grooved girders for which are mounted on the forward end of the rear fuselage, outboard on the roof. The hood is secured in the closed position by a catch lever at the forward end.

The front fuselage is secured to the centre mainplane front spar by bolting the port and starboard vertical portions of the lipped L-section aft former to flanged vertical U-channels mounted on the centre mainplane front spar web. Suitable plate brackets and

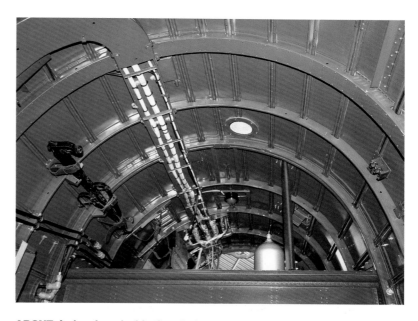

ABOVE A view from inside the wireless operator/air gunner's compartment looking forward. Note the construction of the internal side of the fuselage. *(Jarrod Cotter)*

BELOW Drawings from AP1530 illustrating the Blenheim Mk I fuselage. *(Air Ministry)*

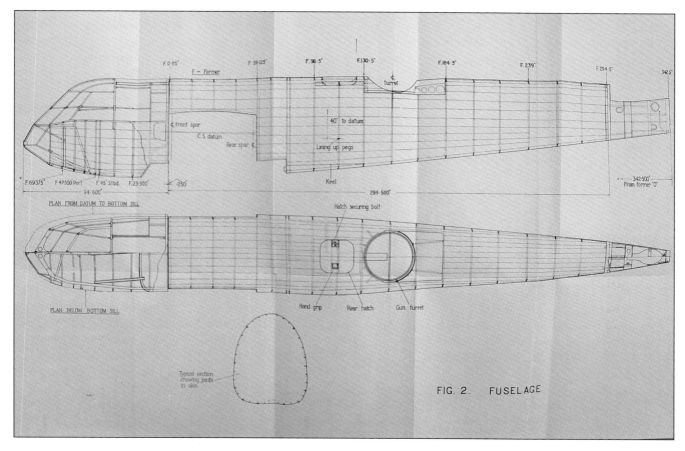

mountings provide for the attachment of the pilot's control chassis, cockpit floor and the various controls.

The port and starboard aft side panels are constructed to permit emergency exits. Each of these panels, when in place, is registered at its top edge and secured at the bottom edge by means of a hand-operated catch lever. When this lever on either panel is lifted clear of its securing pegs, the panel may be pushed outboard from the bottom, on which action the whole panel will fall away clear of the aeroplane.

ABOVE General access to and exit from the cockpit is gained through the transversely rounded sliding transparent hood on the roof, which slides aft to open, as seen here. (Jarrod Cotter)

BELOW A removable panel in the nose of the fuselage, on the starboard side immediately below the bomb-aimer's seat, provides an emergency exit for the pilot and navigator or bomb-aimer. This panel can be operated either from inside or outside the aeroplane by means of T-handles, and is seen removed in this view of L6739, which highlights its location with reference to the navigator/bomb-aimer's seat. (Jarrod Cotter)

BELOW A period view of a Blenheim Mk I cockpit. (Bristol)

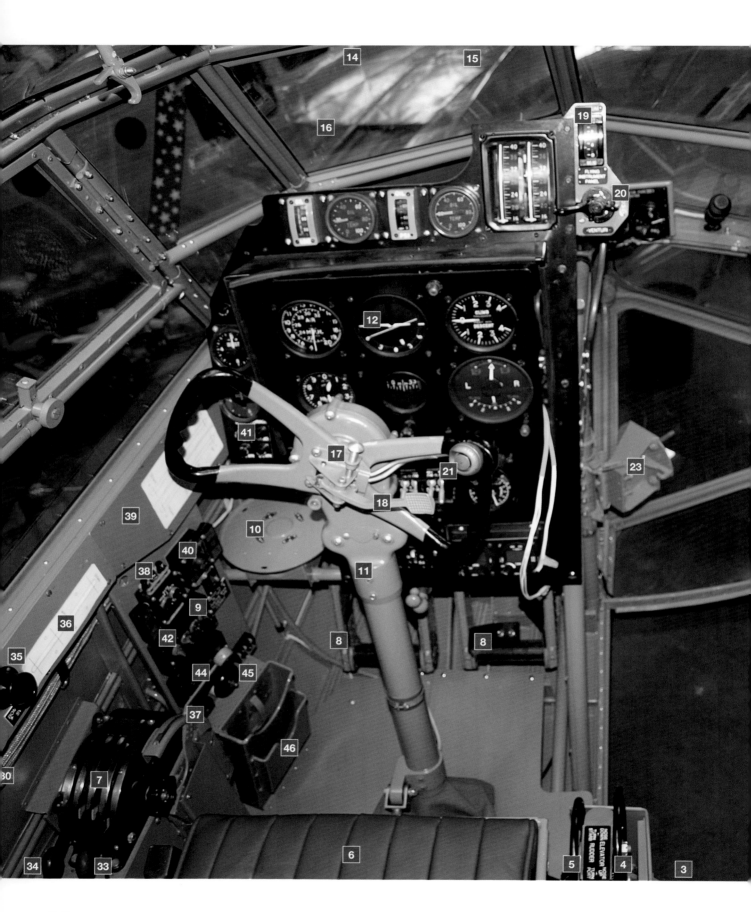

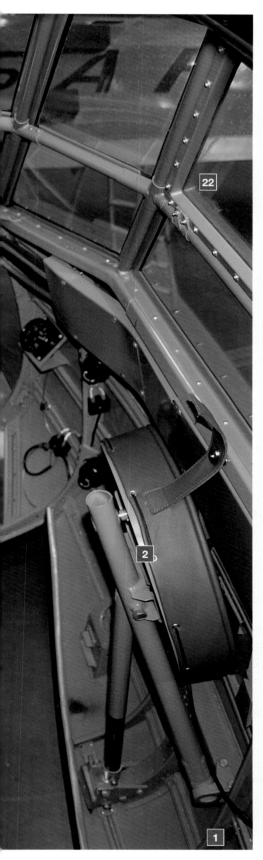

Views of main instrument panel and controls of a Blenheim Mk I.

1 Signal pistol firing tube (not seen)
2 Bomb-aimer's seat
3 Hydraulic hand pump handle (not seen)
4 Elevator trimming tab handwheel
5 Rudder trimming tab handwheel
6 Pilot's seat
7 Engine controls
8 Rudder pedals
9 Bomb switches
10 Position for compass (not fitted here)
11 Control column
12 Instrument panel
13 Hinged panel and catch on port side
14 Bead sight (not seen)
15 Clip for securing direct-vision window in closed position (not seen)
16 Direct-vision window
17 Brake operating lever parking lock
18 Brake operating lever
19 Vacuum gauge
20 Vacuum change-over, venture to pump
21 Gun-firing button
22 Hinged panel on starboard side and catch
23 Course setting bomb-sight mounting
24 Position of shield for undercarriage control handle (not fitted here)
25 Undercarriage control handle
26 Flaps control handle
27 Safety harness release lever (not yet fitted)
28 Safety harness (not yet fitted)
29 Oxygen socket (hidden by seat, not seen)
30 Lever for opening port emergency exit window (not seen)
31 Armrest, port (not seen)
32 Landing lamp switch (not seen)
33 Mixture control levers
34 Throttle control levers
35 Bomb-firing switch
36 Flaps position indicator
37 Landing lamp control lever
38 Bomb nose-and-tail fusing switches
39 Compass card holder
40 Bomb-jettison switch
41 Undercarriage position indicators
42 Flare and practice bomb selector switches
43 Flare switch
44 Bomb selector switch
45 Bomb release master switch
46 Cases for maps

RIGHT A later addition to the Blenheim IV was a rearward-firing Browning 0.303in machine gun fitted into a defensive turret below the front fuselage. *(Air Ministry)*

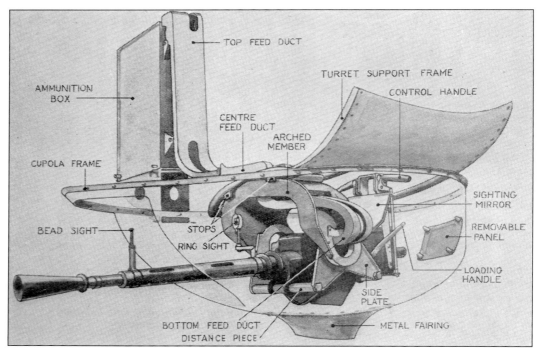

TOP FEED DUCT

TURRET SUPPORT FRAME

CONTROL HANDLE

AMMUNITION BOX

CENTRE FEED DUCT

ARCHED MEMBER

CUPOLA FRAME

SIGHTING MIRROR

REMOVABLE PANEL

BEAD SIGHT

STOPS

RING SIGHT

LOADING HANDLE

SIDE PLATE

BOTTOM FEED DUCT
DISTANCE PIECE

METAL FAIRING

BELOW An illustration showing the observer's method of firing from the forward defensive turret. *(Air Ministry)*

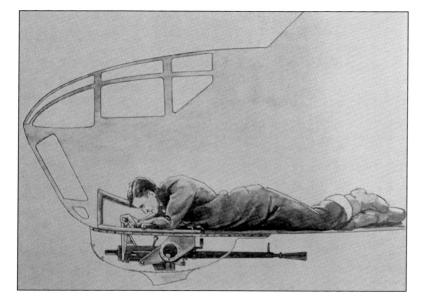

The forward portions of these panels are also designed to slide rearwards, a finger grip being provided at the front edges.

Immediately ahead of the port emergency knock-out panel, a direct vision window is provided. This window is operated by means of a crank handle bevel gear and screw mechanism, mounted immediately below its left-hand bottom corner. The window, opening upwards and outwards, is secured in its closed position by means of a hand-operated scalloped nut and screw which is engaged in a pivot guide block, the crosshead at the outboard end of the screw engaging in a double hook fitting attached to the bottom right-hand corner of the window.

A hinged window is provided on the starboard side of the bomb-aimer's compartment in the nose of the fuselage, and is secured by a sliding bolt at each front and rear bottom corner. These sliding bolts can be secured in their locking position by means of a knurled nut. This window is hinged upwards and inwards; a catch in the underside of the roof securing it in the open position is intended only for ventilation when the aeroplane is on the ground, and should not be opened when in flight. The window should be closed before take-off.

A removable panel in the nose of the fuselage, on the starboard side immediately below the bomb-aimer's seat, provides an emergency exit for the pilot and navigator or bomb-aimer. This panel can be operated either from inside or outside the aeroplane, by means of T-handles housed in recesses in the upper and lower surfaces of the panel, at its starboard edge.

Beneath the extreme forward point of the fuselage nose portion are two transparent panels through which is obtained an unrestricted view below.

Rear fuselage

This portion is constructed of light-alloy flanged U-channel longitudinals, lipped Z-section formers and alclad skin. Access to the main cabin is through a hatch in the cabin roof, at about mid-length, three steps inset into the port side covering giving access to the hole which is provided with a downward-opening door. This door, which is hinged along its port edge, has handgrips above and below its starboard edge and is secured in its closed service position by means of a spring-loaded bolt. Descent into the cabin is made by means of a short vertical ladder secured to the cabin starboard side.

The rear fuselage is secured at its forward upper periphery to the front fuselage as described for the forward fuselage, while the lower portion of the forward end is secured to the centre mainplane top surface and rear spar, flanged U-section verticals being mounted on the aft face of the rear spar web to butt against the front face of the straight side portions of the fuselage bulkhead (59.125in). Below the forward portion of the rear fuselage are two longitudinal bomb compartments, one on each side of the keel, outward-opening spring-loaded double doors being fitted on the underside of each compartment.

Immediately aft of the cabin roof access door is the Bristol gun turret, which rotates on rollers set horizontally and vertically in a segmented U-channel ring bolted to the fuselage structure. The turret ring is of U-section, the

upper rim riding on the horizontally set rollers housed in the fixed segmented ring. From diametrically opposite points on the turret ring are suspended two hollow vertical columns to the feet of which is secured the rotating gun platform. Telescoped into the upper ends of these columns and guided by rollers are tubular members, to the top parts of which is secured the transparent dome. These tubular members and the dome can be raised or lowered by means of the operation crank handle mounted on the port column (with the gun pointing

ABOVE The interior of the wireless operator/air gunner's cabin inside L6739. Note the entrance hatch at top left, and the turret's position at the rear of the compartment. *(Jarrod Cotter)*

FAR LEFT A close-up of the air gunner's seat and the gun turret firing handle. *(Jarrod Cotter)*

LEFT The hinged camera aperture door in the bottom of the fuselage is also for use as an emergency exit for the wireless operator/air gunner. *(Jarrod Cotter)*

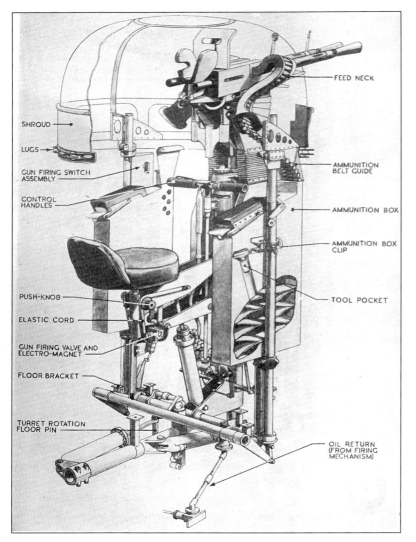

SHROUD

LUGS

GUN FIRING SWITCH
ASSEMBLY

CONTROL
HANDLES

PUSH-KNOB

ELASTIC CORD

GUN FIRING VALVE AND
ELECTRO-MAGNET

FLOOR BRACKET

TURRET ROTATION
FLOOR PIN

FEED NECK

AMMUNITION
BELT GUIDE

AMMUNITION BOX

AMMUNITION BOX
CLIP

TOOL POCKET

OIL RETURN
(FROM FIRING
MECHANISM)

LEFT A drawing of the later Bristol Type BI Mk IV gun turret, armed with two Browning 0.303in machine guns. *(Air Ministry)*

aft). The pinion of the raising and lowering mechanism can be locked by means of a sliding stop in the aft side of the port column, thus securing the hood in either the raised or lowered position. When the gun is being used, the hood should be in its raised position.

The camera aperture is situated in the bottom of the rear fuselage on the starboard side and approximately 3ft 6in aft of the centre mainplane rear spar. The aperture door is rectangular and hinged about its inner longitudinal edge, two wedge action securing levers connected by a tubular handgrip being mounted on the outer longitudinal edge. When the camera is not to be used the aperture door is fitted with a central removable circular window of transparent material. This opening in the bottom of the fuselage is for use as an emergency exit by the wireless operator.

The camera mounting support consists of a tubular stub fixed to the fuselage bottom longitudinal, immediately inboard of the camera aperture. To this stub, the top of which is coned internally, is hinged an upper tubular column, the hinge on the column port side permitting transverse folding of the column horizontally to port. This hinged column, coned at its bottom

RIGHT Internal pictures of the port and starboard bomb compartments. Key: S – outer doors; T – vertical double keel; U – elastic straining chords; V – check cables; W – hinged securing nuts; X – slotted fixings; Y – spring C-clips; Z – plate brackets; A1 – longitudinal support tubes. *(Air Ministry)*

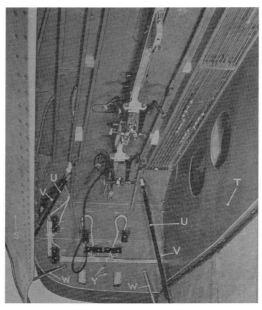

end, is held rigidly in its vertical position by a tubular frame which is hinged longitudinally along the starboard side of the fuselage. At the inboard end of this frame is a knurled disc, the depressing and turning of which releases or engages the frame and column attachment bayonet joint.

Fitted to the camera mounting support upper tubular column is the mounting consisting of a horizontal rectangular frame braced to a vertical tubular sleeve. A binding screw and a spring-loaded peg – which engages one of the holes in the support upper column – permits adjustment of height for the camera mounting.

Immediately aft of the wireless station is a canvas bulkhead, the edges of which are secured to the fuselage former by twine. The bulkhead is in halves to allow passage, the vertical zip-fastener edges of each half permitting the closing of the bulkhead when required.

The bomb doors are fitted to the underside of the fuselage and extend from the fuselage former 12in to former 81in. Two doors are fitted below each port and starboard bomb compartment; the outer doors are shaped to conform to the fuselage and are hinged to the fuselage skin, while the inner doors are hinged to the bottom edge of the vertical double keel. Each inner and outer door consists of a forward and an aft portion, the forward end of the aft portion being tongued between the double cover straps at the

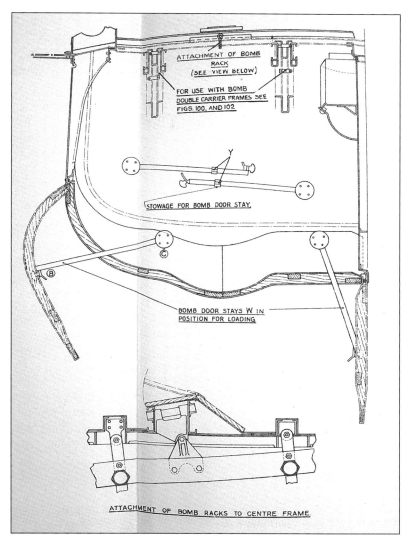

ATTACHMENT OF BOMB RACK (SEE VIEW BELOW)

FOR USE WITH BOMB DOUBLE CARRIER FRAMES SEE FIGS. 100, AND 102

STOWAGE FOR BOMB DOOR STAY.

BOMB DOOR STAYS W IN POSITION FOR LOADING.

ATTACHMENT OF BOMB RACKS TO CENTRE FRAME.

ABOVE A diagram illustrating the bomb-cell doors in their open and closed positions. *(Air Ministry)*

LEFT The Mk IF fighter gun pack fitted to L6739. *(Jarrod Cotter)*

aft ends of the forward portion. The doors are free to open downwards under load and then close automatically by the elastic straining cords, which are provided with check cables. When desired, the doors may be held in their fully open position by means of hinged securing struts, the half-moon swivel heads of the strut free ends engaging slotted attachment fittings on the inner sides of the doors. When disengaged, the struts are stowed in spring C-clips mounted on the ends of the bomb compartment. Immediately above the hinge longitudinal support member of the outer doors are two hinged inspection doors, which are secured by turn-buttons engaging in plate brackets mounted on the longitudinal support tubes.

In the case of L6739 in its Mk IF configuration, the bomb compartment is replaced with a forward-firing gun pack containing four 0.303in Browning machine guns. These are fitted into a box placed below the fuselage in the same position that the bomb bay occupies in a bomber variant.

Stern frame and tail unit

The construction of this portion of the fuselage carries the whole of the tail unit. At the top of this structure, aft of the foremost bulkhead (294.5in), provision is made by a cutaway for receiving the tailplane. The skin at the bottom of the structure was originally cut away to provide

RIGHT Blenheim Mk I L6739's tail unit.
(Jarrod Cotter)

a recess to house the tailwheel when this was made retractable. This feature was not a success and it was consequently covered with an alclad plate.

Between the stern frame foremost bulkhead (294.5in) and the stern post are two transverse frames approximately equally spaced along the stern frame length. The forward intermediate frame is of U-form, a transverse member bridging the frame limb upper ends, the U-frame and bridge piece being of box-section. Bolted to the inside of the U-frame limbs, at the bottom, are the tailwheel oleo leg transverse trunnion support bearings. The aft intermediate frame consists of box-section vertical side members, the top ends of which are bridged. On each side, between the forward intermediate frame and the stern frame forward end, is a longitudinal flanged U-channel which provides support for the elevator control aft countershaft and the tailwheel support lever.

The tail unit consists of a fixed tailplane, a fin, a rudder and elevators, each elevator being fitted with a trimming tab. The rudder and elevators are mass-balanced. The fixed tailplane is built up of two light-alloy channel spars with flanges reinforced by high-tensile steel angles and light-alloy ribs. It is covered with light-alloy sheet. The tailplane tips are separate detachable units attached by set screws. The attachment of the front spar to the stern frame bulkhead is by four bolts, and the rear spar is secured by bolted brackets. An attachment angle on the undersurface at the root is fixed to the fuselage skin by set screws. Where the tailplane butts on the port and starboard sides against the stern frame and the fin, longitudinal fairings are fitted. A bracket on the centre line, aft of the rear spar, carries the centre hinge for the elevators. The elevator outboard hinges are on the outer ends of the main portion of the tailplane.

The fin consists of a leading edge, a rear post, profile formers and alclad skin covering. The rear post extends to the bottom of the stern frame and carries the rudder hinge supports, which are provided with ball races. The screw portion of the rudder trimming tab adjusting mechanism is mounted on the fin rear post. At the bottom of the fin leading edge is fitted a location pin which registers with an eye on the centre line of the fuselage. The skin at the root of the fin is attached to the stern frame and tailplane by means of screws, the fin rear post being secured at its bottom end to the vertically set plate. On the port side the skin is fitted with a circular inspection door to give access to the lubricator on the trimming tab operating gear.

The rudder comprises a light-alloy rudder post, 11 light-alloy plate ribs, a tubular trailing edge and, on its balance portion, an alclad skin covering, the remaining portion of the rudder being fabric covered. The rudder post is of box-section and is built up of two channels, the aft short-lipped channel fitting between the extended lips of the forward channel. At the bottom of the rudder post – one on each side – are mounted eyed fittings to which is secured the rudder operating double armed lever. Doubling plates riveted to the rudder post flanges provide means of attachment for the forward ends of the flanged plate ribs. On the forward face of the rudder post, below the balance portion, is secured the nose fairing, in the top end of which is a horizontal slot which receives the trimming tab double-eyed operating spindle. Inset at the trailing edge is a rudder trimming tab, the hinges of which consist of two U-plates that wrap the vertical member.

Secured to the starboard side of rib No 7 from the top is the trimming tab operating rod guard. At the top of the rudder balance portion is secured the mass-balance weight. Immediately above and below the rudder trimming tab are the tail lamp mountings. The rudder trimming tab is constructed of a thin wedge of wood and is alclad covered. On the starboard side of this tab is bolted the operating lever.

The elevators consist of separate port and starboard units, each of which comprises a steel torque tube, eight single ribs and two box ribs of light-alloy plate construction, a tubular trailing edge, a leading edge of U-section light-alloy sheet and a nose fairing. The elevator balance portions are metal covered, the remaining portions of the elevators being fabric covered. Mounted at the inner end of each elevator torque tube is an operating lever, the two levers when bolted together forming the interconnection of the port and starboard elevator torque tubes. The centre hinge of the elevators consists of a spigot at the inner end of

each torque tube engaging the corresponding port and starboard sides of a ball race, centrally mounted on the tailplane rear spar. The outer hinges, consisting of split bearings, are bolted to the brackets mounted on the aft portion of the outer ends of the tailplane main section.

Elevator trimming tabs, positioned inboard of the trailing edge extension piece of each elevator, are of light-alloy construction. Each trimming tab is supported at three hinge points, the hinges consisting of U-section plate fittings which wrap the elevator tubular trailing edge. Mounted on the underside of each tab is an operating lever, while on the underside of each elevator, below the fourth and fifth ribs from the inner end, is mounted the operating link guard.

Mainplanes

The mainplane consists of three portions: the centre mainplane and the port and starboard outer mainplanes. The centre portion of the undersurface of the centre mainplane constitutes the floor at the forward end of the main cabin portion of the fuselage through which the centre mainplane front and rear spars are continuous. At the outboard ends of the centre mainplane are mounted the engine nacelles and undercarriage structures. The outer mainplanes have flotation compartments formed by sealing the space between the main spars.

To the centre and outer plane trailing edges are fitted hydraulically operated flaps outboard of which are the ailerons. Below the centre mainplane, provision is made for carrying

ABOVE A detail close-up showing the positioning of the rudder and starboard elevator trim tabs. Note that on this side is the rudder trim tab operating lever. *(Jarrod Cotter)*

RIGHT L6739 in the
ARC hangar. This
high-level view shows
the aircraft's general
layout well.
(Jarrod Cotter)

BELOW Inside the
airframe, situated
centrally between the
spars, is a well. In the
floor of this, above the
bomb compartment
and out of sight in
this view, is a small
longitudinally hinged
door which gives
access to the elevator
and rudder control
cable strainers.
(Jarrod Cotter)

bombs, and a Browning gun is housed in the port outer plane. Provision is also made for fitting two landing lamps in the leading edge of the port outer plane.

The centre mainplane is, in plan, symmetrical about its centre line; its ribs, transverse stiffeners and spar webs being of alclad, while the front and rear spar booms and attachment end fittings are high-tensile steel. The covering is of alclad for both upper and lower surfaces, provision being made on the stiffened undersurface of the centre portion for securing the bomb carriers or the bomb carrier frames, which enable two bombs to be carried abreast in each bomb compartment. Housing for two flares is provided at the inboard end of each port and starboard trailing edge portion of this plane.

At the outboard ends of this plane, between the front and rear spars, is provided the housing for the engine mounting and undercarriage structure. Immediately inboard of this housing and between the spars are located the main fuel tanks, one each on the port and starboard sides. Centrally between the spars is provided a well, in the floor of which (above the bomb compartment), is a small longitudinally hinged door which gives access to the elevator and rudder control cable strainers.

The front and rear spars are, in general, similar in their construction, each consisting of an alclad web and build-up top and bottom high-tensile steel booms. The spar booms are of laminated angle-section construction, with laminated cornices at each top and bottom, front and rear boom angle, running the full length of the spars. The front spar boom aft, and the rear spar boom forward angles have two laminations only for the portion of the spar 5ft 10in on each side of the centre line; the outer lengths of these angles, together with the whole length of the front spar boom forward and the rear spar boom aft angles, have three laminations.

Spar end fittings for the front and rear spar joints consist of two transverse-eyed bar fittings on the forward and aft sides of each boom, top and bottom outer links and centre links, besides two vertical reinforcing channels. The bottom centre link for the front spar is in the form of a 'D'.

The ribs are of alclad construction, those adjacent to the fuselage being of box form. The ribs consist of three portions, viz. the nose portion, centre portion (the ends of which abut the front and rear spars) and the trailing edge portion. The trailing edge portion of these ribs are shaped at their trailing edges to take the hydraulically operated flaps.

The engine mounting support structures are positioned at the ends of the centre mainplane, between the front and rear spars, and provide means of attachment for the engine mountings and the folding undercarriage. Each structure consists of two longitudinal triangulated frames transversely connected. The frame members are constructed of square-section high-tensile steel tubes, the ends of which are sandwiched between finger plates and rigidly secured by through-bolts. The longitudinal frames, as a unit, are held together at their panel points by tubular transverse members, the forward top panel point being doubly held by a second transverse tubular member which provides support for the main oil tank at its forward end. The structure top horizontal and forward transverse diagonal panels are cross-braced by tie-rods.

The aft end of each frame is provided with a rigidly secured light-alloy bracket of double T-form, the bracket flanges being bolted to a lightened box-section vertical plate support mounted on the forward face of the rear spar web. The forward vertical members of each engine mounting structure are secured to the forward face of the front spar web by means of

vertical double U-brackets, the vertical members being secured between the forward-pointing limbs of the U-brackets by through-bolts.

Immediately below the frame centre panel bottom joints, at mid-length of the structure, are

ABOVE Blenheim Mk IV L4842 shows off its wing plan well. Note the position of the engine mountings, the joints between the wing centre section and the two outer sections, the ailerons on each outer trailing edge, the landing lights on the port outer leading edge and the navigation and formation lights on each wingtip. *(Bristol)*

LEFT The aperture for the fixed Browning machine-gun muzzle fitted in the port wing covered with red fabric tape sealing. When the aircraft returned from a sortie, if the red seal was broken armourers would know that the gun had been fired. *(Jarrod Cotter)*

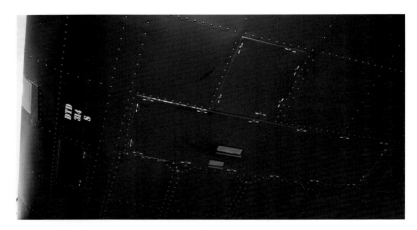

ABOVE An access door for the Browning machine gun in the port wing is provided on the wing's undersurface. The securing points are clearly visible. *(Jarrod Cotter)*

provided bearings which support the ends of the undercarriage radius rod transverse torque shaft. The structure transverse vertical panel, of which the torque shaft is the bottom member, is braced by means of tubular struts between points at approximately one-third of the torque tube length and the upper and lower central panel points of each longitudinal frame. The front transverse panel of this nacelle structure is

BELOW The hydraulically operated flaps are in four sections, the port and starboard centre mainplane flaps, and the port and starboard outer mainplane flaps. However, all operate simultaneously. *(Jarrod Cotter)*

held structurally rigid to the front spar top and bottom booms by tubular struts which are pin-jointed to double-eyed T-brackets positioned on the nacelle centre line and mounted below the bottom and above the top booms of the front spar. Below the structure front bottom panel points, provision is made by means of double-plate lipped brackets for the attachment of the upper ends of the inner and outer oleo-legs.

Each of the outer mainplanes consists of front and rear spars, 17 ribs and a plane tip, the upper and lower surface covering being of alclad sheet. Housed at the inboard end of each outer plane, between the front and rear spars, is a long-range fuel tank. At the inboard portion of the trailing edge of each plane is fitted a hydraulically operated outer split flap, while at the outboard portion is fitted an aileron.

In the port outer plane is housed a fixed Browning 0.303in machine gun, a specially constructed gun mounting being provided between the front and rear spars. This gun mounting consists of two parallel longitudinal tubes rigidly intercoupled by two transverse sleeve mountings and two plates. The forward and aft ends of these tubes are pin-jointed to lug fittings which are secured to plate brackets mounted on the aft and forward faces of the front and rear spars respectively. The web of the front spar is cut away, in line horizontally with the centre line of the gun mounting, and an access door secured at 14 to 16 points, is provided on the undersurface of the wing, immediately below.

In construction the front and rear spars are similar to those of the centre mainplane front and rear spars, each spar consisting of an alclad web with laminated top and bottom angle booms. The number of laminations composing the front and rear angles of the top and bottom booms decreases in the run outboard.

Spar end fittings are, in general, similar to those of the centre plane front and rear spar end fittings, the sandwich plate, links and vertical reinforcing plate being common to the outer plane front and rear spar inboard end fittings.

These ribs consist of three portions, viz. the nose portion, the centre portion and the trailing edge portion, and are constructed of alclad, the ribs being lipped at their top and bottom edges and lightened. In each plane are 17 ribs;

ribs Nos 1, 9, 13 and 17 from the inboard end being of box form.

Wingtips are constructed of lightened longitudinal and transverse formers secured to the U-section profile edge. The tip covering is of alclad, the inboard edge lapping over the joggled outboard edge of the mainplane covering and being bolted to the outer plane end box rib booms.

At two points on the profile edge of each plane tip two formation-keeping lamps are housed. Double landing lamps are also provided in the nose portion of the outer mainplane.

Ailerons

The ailerons, which are aerodynamically and statically balanced, are constructed of ten light-alloy ribs which are carried on a high-tensile steel torque tube. On this torque tube, between the ribs, are also mounted eight nose-portion formers. The leading edge is made of spruce, the trailing edge being of magnesium alloy. The aileron inboard and outboard hinges consist of ball races mounted at the ends of the aileron torque tube, the double-eyed hinge pin being secured to the mainplanes. The centre hinge consists of a split bearing which is secured to a bracket on the mainplanes. The aileron operating lever is mounted on the torque tube, approximately at mid-length, near the centre hinge. About mid-length of the trailing edge is a trimming tab. The ailerons are fabric covered.

Aileron trimming tabs, on both port and starboard ailerons, are constructed of light-alloy sheet and are secured to the aileron by means of a thin strip of stainless steel which functions as a hinge. A differential quadrant and locking plate allow ground adjustment of the trimming tab. The port and starboard trimming tabs should be initially set to zero incidence to the ailerons. When difficulty is experienced in correcting the tendency of the aeroplane to fly left wing or right wing low, it is necessary to fit new trimming tabs of increased chord to the port and starboard ailerons.

Flaps

The hydraulically operated flaps are in four sections in all: the port and starboard centre mainplane flaps, and the port and starboard outer mainplane flaps. All are simultaneously operated. They are of the split type and constructed of light-alloy and magnesium alloy sheet, and are hinged on a hollow rod. The centre mainplane flaps are recessed at their inboard end forward portions to give clearance for the flare compartment downward-opening doors. The flap hinges are carried on support structures which are attached to the centre and outer mainplanes at each rib position.

Undercarriage

The undercarriage consists of two independent units positioned 7ft 9in from the centre line of the aeroplane, and in line longitudinally with the engine nacelles. Each unit consists essentially of a wheel, a folding transverse frame and two knee-jointed radius rods; the wheel axle constitutes the bottom member of the frame and the shock-absorbing oleo-legs the side members, these being cross-braced by tubular members. The undercarriage units are retractable, the two units being simultaneously raised or lowered by hydraulically operated jacks.

The raising and lowering of each undercarriage is effected by means of a sturdy braced transverse panel which is pivoted at the top ends of its oleo-leg side members. The

LEFT A close-up of the port mainwheel showing the build of the unit. *(Jarrod Cotter)*

RIGHT This view of the port main-wheel unit shows the fairing door, which leaves part of the tyre exposed when the undercarriage is retracted.
(Jarrod Cotter)

panel transverse bracing consists of a star fitting on each side of which are two socket branches. The converging ends of the tubular cross bracing are secured in these socket branches by taper pins, the other ends of the bracing members being fixed by single bolts to lugs integral with the oleo-leg cylinders. The lower end of the hydraulic operating jack piston rod is attached by a single bolt to the crosshead on the oleo assembly. The axle is secured at its ends in hinged cap supports at the oleo-leg sustaining rams. Transversely connecting the oleo-legs at their ends is a reinforcing girder to which the star fitting is fastened by two bolts. The oleo-legs are braced in their down position by the knee-jointed radius rods, the upper ends

of which are splined to the outer ends of the main torque shaft.

Mounted at the middle of the torque shaft are twin levers carrying trunnion bearings for the operating hydraulic jack. The bottom end of the piston rod of the jack is connected to the star fitting, while the jack trunnions at its mid-length are pivoted by the twin levers. Locking catches for the undercarriage retracted and down positions on the inner sides of the radius rods are connected vertically by pin-jointed struts, while the upper (or retracting) catches are rigidly mounted on a transverse auxiliary torque shaft. This shaft, operated by a hydraulic locking jack, releases the undercarriage 'engaged' locking catches and resets the 'free' locking catches for engagements. An additional function of these locking jacks is the controlling (i.e. timing) of the admission of pressure to the undercarriage main retracting jacks. Until the catches are completely withdrawn, pressure cannot be admitted to the retracting jacks owing to the obscuring of the ports in the locking jacks by the pistons which are integral with the locking jack operating spindles.

The oleo-legs are oleo-pneumatic in their action, compressed air being the energising medium and oil the damping medium. The oil is maintained at a level determined by the position of the bottom of the oil-level tube. On the compression stroke the air above the oil is compressed and the oil reservoir in the upper end of the sustaining ram shrouds the plunger secured to the top of the cylinder, the plunger displacing oil from the reservoir through the annular channel between the shoulder at the top of the reservoir and the wall of the plunger. The plunger, being tapered, causes a progressive restriction in the annular channel to the escaping oil. This restriction creates an increasing damping resistance superimposed on the resistance of the further-compressed air. A secondary means of escape for the oil in the reservoir is through the small intercommunicating hole in the bottom of the hollow plunger.

On the ground, the effective air pressure on the pistons of the oleo-legs balances, in greater part, the weight of the aeroplane. Before subjecting the oleo-legs to the aeroplane weight, each oleo-leg must be charged with

BELOW This image from AP1530 illustrates a mainwheel unit in its retracted position.
(Air Ministry)

dry air to the pressure stated on the instruction plate, i.e. 400lb/in². The correct oil content is 2.1 pints of oil, anti-freezing, type A (Stores Ref 34A/43 and 46). The maximum extension of the oleo-legs is 6in, and the legs are so designed that under normal static load the approximate extension is 4.5in.

Safety locks

In the earlier aeroplanes, in order to prevent the undercarriage being retracted when the aeroplane is on the ground (due to inadvertent working of the hand pump with the selector valve set for undercarriage retraction), ground safety links are provided. These links, stowed in the fuselage just aft of the hatchway ladder during flight, are attached on to the inner legs of the port and starboard units, at the neck of the top fitting of the oleo strut and above the centre line of the radius rod knee joint. An adjuster is fitted to the link for setting to the correct length on assembly. These links should always be attached when the aeroplane is stationary on the airfield or in a hangar. A red streamer is fixed on each link to enable the pilot to see from the cockpit if the link has been left in position before taking off.

In later aeroplanes an automatic locking device is provided to prevent the undercarriage being retracted when the aeroplane is on the ground, due to the inadvertent working of

the hand pump with the selector valve set for undercarriage retraction. This device is fitted to the outboard leg of each undercarriage unit. A horizontal plunger mounted on the undercarriage radius rod registers, when the undercarriage is extended, in a hole in a cylinder which is secured to the oleo-leg. On landing, and while the aeroplane is on the ground, the oleo-leg is compressed. This compression movement is transmitted, by means of the push and pull rod, to the vertical plunger, which engages in the vertically set hole in the horizontal plunger. This securing of the horizontal plunger prevents the radius rods from folding in response to the torque induced in the torque tube by the inadvertent applied retraction effort of the hydraulic jack.

Brakes

Each port and starboard brake unit is of the Dunlop type and consists of a rimmed disc which is bolted to the brake unit torque flange integral with the inboard sleeve on the axle. The undercarriage wheel brake system comprises two pneumatic brake units, a Dunlop-type dual relay valve, with link and lever control mechanism and operating cable, a triple air-pressure gauge and necessary tubing and couplings.

The brake hand lever on the control column handwheel governs, by means of the Bowden cable, the air supply to the relay valve, which

ABOVE L6739 with its main wheels retracted while in flight close to Duxford. Note how the tyres remain partially exposed. *(Jarrod Cotter)*

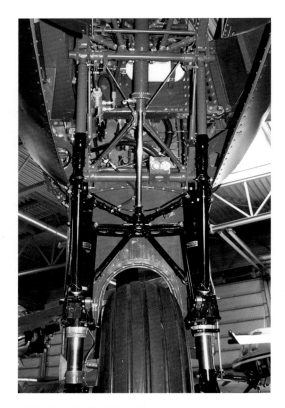

RIGHT A detail picture showing the inner workings and pipework which operate the retractable mainwheel and its brake system.
(Jarrod Cotter)

RIGHT The main undercarriage lamp indicators in the pilot's cockpit. When the aeroplane is in flight and the undercarriage retracted, a red light (top) shows for each wheel unit. When the undercarriage unit is being lowered the corresponding red light is automatically switched off, and a corresponding green light (bottom) is switched on when the undercarriage unit is fully down and the locking catch is engaged.
(Jarrod Cotter)

RIGHT The castoring non-retractable tailwheel on L6739.
(Jarrod Cotter)

controls – either differentially or simultaneously – the air pressure supply to the brakes. When the rudder pedals are in their neutral position, the movement of the hand lever to the 'on' position ensures an equal air pressure supply to both port and starboard wheel brake units simultaneously. The differential functioning of the relay valve is dependent on the 'displaced from neutral' position of the rudder pedals, the relay valve operating lever being coupled by means of two horizontally set levers and two links with the rudder control vertical torque tube.

Warning devices

Switches working with the locking catches operate lamp indicators in the pilot's cockpit. When the aeroplane is in flight and the undercarriage retracted, a red light shows for each wheel unit. When the undercarriage unit is being lowered, the corresponding red light is automatically switched off, and a corresponding green light is switched on when the undercarriage unit is fully down and the locking catch is engaged. The green light remains on until it is cut out by a switch coupled to the engine switch on the instrument panel.

An electrical buzzer in the nose of the aeroplane sounds if the throttle levers are moved back more than two-thirds of the way from the fully open position with the undercarriage retracted. The buzzer remains in operation with the throttle levers in this position so long as the undercarriage remains fully retracted. The throttle buzzer switches are interconnected electrically with those for the top undercarriage catches, so that the red lights and the buzzer go out of operation simultaneously when the units commence to lower.

In a longitudinal conduit on the port side of the pilot's cockpit is fitted a mechanically operated indicator. It is actuated by the splined torque shaft of the undercarriage mechanism and shows the intermediate positions of the undercarriage in between their fully lowered and fully retracted positions, when the warning lamps are switched off.

Tailwheel unit

The tailwheel unit is non-retracting and consists of a wheel, a tubular steel fork provided at its ends with towing eyes and an oleo-pneumatic or a spring-oleo shock-absorbing leg which constitutes the tailwheel unit stem. The tailwheel has a fully castoring action.

The tailwheel has a Dunlop-type 'Ecta' WL11 heavy tyre, of 5.5in width × 4in wheel-rim diameter. The hub (Dunlop AHO 5007, 4in width × 4in diameter) is fitted with ball bearings.

Flying controls

The aeroplane is controlled from the port side of the pilot's cockpit, but may also be operated from the starboard side if dual controls are fitted. The aileron and elevator controls consist of the conventional type of wheel control column, the rudder controls being pedal-operated. The aileron control mechanism allows differential movement and each aileron has an inset trimming tab which is provided with means for ground adjustment. The elevators and rudder are also provided with trimming tabs which are operated from the cockpit, the rudder trimming tab also having automatic servo action. Automatic controls for the control surfaces are fitted and the mainplane flaps are hydraulically operated.

Pilot's control chassis

This structure is of tubular construction, the longitudinal side frames being transversely connected at their base by tubular members, and at their forward and aft ends by the control column support beams and the braced vertical transverse frame respectively. The structure unit bottom longitudinal members are secured to the cockpit floor inverted U-section longitudinals by through-bolts, the rear vertical frame being secured on the forward side of the front spar. Supported by each side frame, at approximately one-third of its height, is a hand-controlled torque tube on which are mounted two forward-pointing levers. Pivoted to the ends of these levers is the first pilot's seat, which is secured at the back top corners by the links. At the port side of the structure is a plate quadrant, the inner arc of which is scalloped to receive the seat height-adjusting hand-lever bolt, the hand-lever being spring-loaded. To disengage the locking bolt the height-adjusting lever handgrip is turned counter-clockwise (looking forward) when an internal profiled sleeve forces down

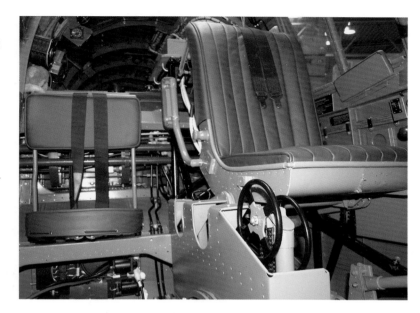

an internal spring-loaded spindle to which the engagement bolt is secured. Elastic straining cords relieve the levers of the weight of the seat occupant, thus facilitating adjustment. Supported by two vertical bridge plates at the control chassis forward end is the elevator and rudder control front countershaft, while at the chassis forward end is the control column support beam.

Control column

The control column consists of a light-alloy tube, at the top and bottom ends of which are light-alloy socket mountings. In the top socket mounting, which comprises a front and a rear portion, is the handwheel spindle. This spindle is built up of two shouldered collars mounted on a splined central sleeve, the collars being housed in bushes. To the rear collar integral

ABOVE The pilot's control chassis is seen to the right of this picture with the seat mounted to it. Next to this, seen at the left of the picture, is the navigator/bomb-aimer's seat.
(Jarrod Cotter)

BELOW A close-up of L6739's control handwheel, on which is mounted the brake-operating lever.
(Jarrod Cotter)

flange is secured the control handwheel, on which is attached the brake-operating lever. Mounted on the handwheel splined sleeve between the front and the rear portions of the control column head is the aileron control sprocket, below which, in the control column head and in line with the sprocket periphery, are secured two chain guides.

The control column foot sock mounting is trunnioned, the trunnions being supported by side plates which are held rigidly together at their forward end by a transverse plate. Aft of the trunnion axis, the side plates provide lugs which house the aileron control ball-bearing sprocket support spindle, on which are mounted collared distance tubes. A hollow bolt in conjunction with the distance tubes registers the aft ends of the side plates. Through this hollow bolt is inserted the pivot bolt, which secures the control column to the transverse beam at the forward end of the pilot's control chassis.

Dual controls

For training purposes dual controls can be fitted, comprising a second pilot's control handwheel, control column, rudder pedals and triangular rudder bar lever on the starboard side of the cockpit, in line transversely with those of the first pilot. Movements of the second pilot's control column are passed to

RIGHT **The dual-control adaption fitted to some Blenheims for pilot training.**
(Air Ministry)

the first pilot's control column by means of a transverse torque tube.

Movements of the second pilot's handwheel are transmitted to that of the first pilot by means of the control handwheel spindle sprockets and a transverse chain, each top and bottom portion of which is enclosed in a tube connecting the first and second pilots' control column heads. The lower tube is rotatable to facilitate adjustment of the chain.

The second pilot's controls constitute a complete unit, which comprises a portable supporting floor and a longitudinal main member, in the aft end of which is pivoted the second pilot's control column, and at the forward end is pivoted the rudder bar lever. Pin-jointed to the ends of the rudder bar lever are longitudinal pedal support tubes in the aft ends of which are telescoped the stems of the adjustable T-pedals. The aft ends of the pedal support tubes are connected by a pivoted transverse tube, which, in conjunction with the rudder bar, permits parallel fore-and-aft pedal movement. Pin-jointed to the forward end of the rudder bar is a transverse rod, to the port end of which is pin-jointed the rudder torque tube lever, which in turn is mounted on the double-collared sleeve on the first pilot's rudder vertical torque tube. A brake control relay cable is led from its actuating lever on the starboard portion of the control column top transverse connecting tube to the dual control link in the first pilot's brake control cable.

Aileron controls

The control handwheel movement is transmitted by means of the chains and tie-rods to the bottom ends of the double-armed levers, the top ends of which are coupled by the connecting rod. Connecting rods are led outboard along the forward face of the front spar to the differential bell crank lever, pin-jointed support being provided by the vertically set support lever and the horizontally set support levers.

From the differential bell crank lever a longitudinal connecting rod is taken to the longitudinally set lever to which is coupled the universal end of the link. The aft end of this link is pin-jointed to the aileron operating lever.

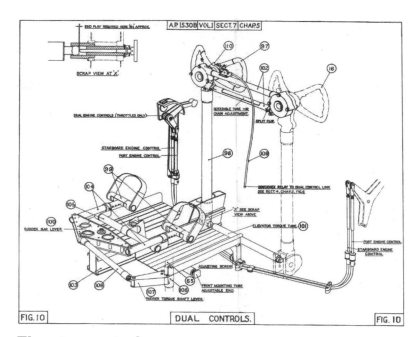

Elevator controls

The fore and aft movement of the control column is transmitted to the pilot's chassis forward countershaft sleeve by means of the connecting link, the forward and aft ball-bearing ends of which are respectively connected to the control column rigged mounting and the sleeve lever. From the ends of the countershaft sleeve levers duplicated 15cwt cables are led over the corresponding pulleys in the group mounted on the forward side of the bomb well, thence over a second group and under

ABOVE A diagram showing how the Blenheim dual-control system was connected to the first pilot's controls. *(Air Ministry)*

BELOW Flying control joint and cable assemblies at the point below the pilot's seat. *(Jarrod Cotter)*

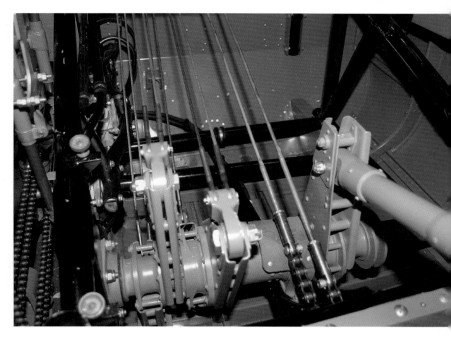

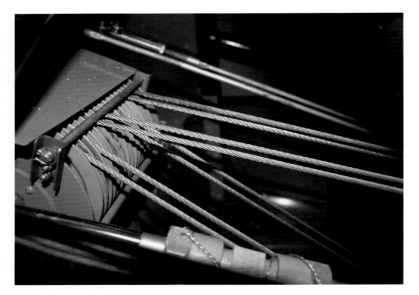

ABOVE **The flying control pulley point in front of the bomb bay.**
(Jarrod Cotter)

BELOW **The rudder pedals are of stirrup form, with leather foot-securing straps provided above the pedal footrests in the lever forks.**
(Jarrod Cotter)

countershaft lever. The duplicated cables from the bottom lever engage the next outboard pair of pulleys of the pulley groups, and are then led to the bottom arm of the lever.

Rudder controls

The rudder operating pedal levers are freely suspended on the transverse support tube which is secured to the fuselage nose portion port side and the centrally positioned support frame. The pedals are of stirrup form, leather foot-securing straps being provided above the pedals in the pedal lever forks. Coupled to each pedal lever, at approximately mid-length, is a ball-bearing ended link, the forward end of which is connected to a transverse rudder bar. This rudder bar is secured to the vertical torque tube by an adjustable crosshead by means of which the pedals may be adjusted to a limit of 3in forward and aft of their normal extreme positions when the crosshead is at its mid-travel. This adjustment is affected by the operation of the crank at the aft end of the crosshead extension spindle.

At the bottom of the vertical torque tube is secured an inboard-pointing lever coupled to which is the forward ball-bearing end of the longitudinal connecting rod. The aft end of this rod is attached to the downward-pointing lever secured to the front countershaft sleeve. From this lever and from the upward-pointing lever, also secured to the sleeve, duplicated 15cwt cables are led parallel, in their run aft to the fuselage former, to the elevator duplicated cables, which are engaged by the same pulley groups. Aft of the pulley group the rudder cables are led through fairleads to the rudder double-armed operating lever. The duplicated cables from the rudder control front countershaft bottom lever engage the inboard pair of pulleys of the pulley groups and are then led to the starboard end of the rudder operating lever. The duplicated cables from the top lever engage the next inboard pair of pulleys of the pulley groups and are then led to the port end of the operating lever.

a third group of pulleys mounted aft of the bomb well. The cables continue in their run aft under the four outboard pulleys of the eight-pulley group mounted at the bottom of the fuselage former, then to the ends of the vertical double-armed lever secured to the transverse countershaft. Centrally mounted on this countershaft is an upward-pointing lever. To this lever is pin-jointed the forward end of the longitudinal connecting rod, the aft end of which is coupled to the elevator operating lever. The duplicated cables from the elevator control front countershaft top lever engage the outboard pair of pulleys of the pulley groups and are then led to the top arm of the elevator control rear

Elevator and rudder trimming tab controls

These controls are similar and run in parallel from the pilot's cockpit trimming tab control

handwheels to the fuselage stern frame. The elevator and rudder trimming tab control handwheels respectively, are mounted at the top of a vertical column secured to the pilot's control chassis, immediately forward and to starboard of the pilot's seat. Each control handwheel movement is transmitted by means of the corresponding chain or to corresponding double sprockets or mounted immediately below. From the aft ends of the longitudinal chains and 5cwt cables are led aft through fairleads, engaging in their run aft seven groups of quadruple pulleys. The sixth pulley group, from forward, is horizontally set, the remaining groups being vertically set. The cables for the elevator trimming tab controls engage the port pair of pulleys, and the cables for the rudder trimming tab controls engage the starboard pair of pulleys.

Flap controls

The flaps are actuated by a single hydraulically operated jack, mounted in the centre mainplane on the port side. The forward lug of this jack is pin-jointed to a bracket secured to the forward end of the centre mainplane rib No 4. The ram consists of a tube, at the aft end of which is an adjustable-eyed screwed fitting, secured by a lock nut. At the forward end of the ram is secured a piston, the sealing of which is effected by four U-shaped leather packing rings.

Between tail ribs Nos 2 and 4 of the centre mainplane, on each port and starboard side, is mounted a quadrant lever, the port of which provides means of a pin-jointed attachment for the aft end of the hydraulic ram. From the two forward cable attachment points of each quadrant, 45cwt cables, common to both quadrants, are led forward over double pulleys mounted immediately aft of the rear spar at tail rib No 3 and thence transversal inboard. To the forward ends of the quadrants are coupled links, the outboard ends of which are connected to the eyed sleeves mounted on the inner operating tubes. The outer and inner flap operating tubes are coupled by the link, with bearing support to the tubes being provided at the rib stations of the flap hinge structure. Toggle links, pin-jointed at their upper ends to corresponding eyed sleeves on the operating tubes, are coupled at their lower ends to the split flap attachment eyes.

Engine installation

The Blenheim's power is provided by two Bristol Mercury engines (of varying marks depending on when fitted), each carried at the centre plane leading edge by a nacelle attached to the front and rear spars. Two main fuel tanks are fitted in the centre plane and one long-range tank in each outer plane (Mk IV) between the front and rear spars. The fuel in the outer tanks can be jettisoned. In each nacelle are mounted a main and an auxiliary oil tank, as well as an oil cooler.

The engine installations are entirely independent, but the fuel tanks on each side

LEFT The elevator and rudder trimming tab control handwheels are mounted at the top of a vertical column secured to the pilot's control chassis, immediately forward and to starboard of the pilot's seat. Each control handwheel movement is transmitted by means of the corresponding chains, which are visible running down and then behind the point of control. *(Jarrod Cotter)*

BELOW One of L6739's Bristol Mercury XX engines seen in August 2014 shortly before being fitted to the Blenheim. *(Jarrod Cotter)*

of the aeroplane are inter-coupled – both for suction and delivery – by balance pipes, each of which is fitted with a cock having a remote control. The fuel supply is maintained by engine-driven pumps and by gravity. If necessary, by operating the balance control cocks, each pump can draw from either main tank or either long-range tank, and each pump can supply both engines.

A high initial oil pressure device incorporated in the oil pump ensures an adequate supply of oil for the vital parts of the engine when the oil is cold, and allows the aeroplane to take off soon after the engines are started. In cold weather the period normally required for warming up is considerably reduced by a partial circulation chamber incorporated in the oil tank.

The engine cowling at the trailing edge is fitted with controllable gills that govern the engine cooling. The exhaust collector forms the leading edge of the cowling. The engine may be started either electrically or by hand.

The throttle and mixture controls for the port and starboard engines, including the controls for the carburettor cut-out, the air-intake shutter and the propellers, are independent, and are mounted on plate brackets in pairs, so that the port and starboard controls can be operated simultaneously if desired.

Engine mountings

Each engine mounting consists of a steel tubular structure carrying a flanged engine ring and a firewall. This mounting is attached, as a unit, to the front end of the engine mounting structure. The engine is secured to the engine mounting ring by 18 bolts, with Duralumin packing blocks, slotted nuts and split pins fitted behind the flange of the ring. The lower end of the ring has a detachable segment to facilitate changing the engine without removing the carburettor. The nacelle fairing is constructed of aluminium panels which are mounted on steel tubular framing. An electrical generator, attached to the outboard side of the port nacelle on the engine mounting, is fitted with air inlet and outlet tubes which are flush with the side panel in the fairing. An engine-speed indicator electrical generator, connected to the engine by a flexible drive

ABOVE A comparison view showing one Mercury engine with its cylinder heads fitted, and another which has yet to have its pistons and cylinder heads installed.
(Jarrod Cotter)

RIGHT The engine cowl gills seen in the open position.
(Jarrod Cotter)

and by an electrical lead to the indicator in the cockpit, is clipped to the starboard diagonal of each engine mounting.

Propellers

De Havilland variable-pitch metal three-bladed, metal propellers are fitted to the engines (further details including pitch angles are given in Chapter 2). The engine oil pressure is employed for changing the pitch from coarse to fine, while a set of counterweights return the blades to coarse pitch when oil pressure is released from the system. The pitch control valve is located on the port side of the rear cover of the engine and consists of a two-position plunger operated by a remote control in the cockpit.

Fuel system

The fuel system is of the gravity type, engine-driven fuel pumps also being provided. On a Blenheim, fuel for both engines is contained in two main and two long-range tanks, each main and long-range tank having a capacity of 140 and 94 gallons respectively. The main tanks are mounted between the front and rear spars of the centre plane, one on each side of the fuselage inboard of the engine nacelles, while the long-range tanks are similarly mounted in the outer mainplanes. Each tank is strapped to bearers riveted to detachable

LEFT The engine mountings consist of a steel tubular structure carrying a flanged engine ring and a firewall. They are attached, as a unit, to the front end of each engine mounting structure.
(Jarrod Cotter)

LEFT L6739 is fitted with variable-pitch de Havilland three-bladed, metal propellers.
(Jarrod Cotter)

LEFT A close-up of the Blenheim's propeller hub and blade combination.
(Jarrod Cotter)

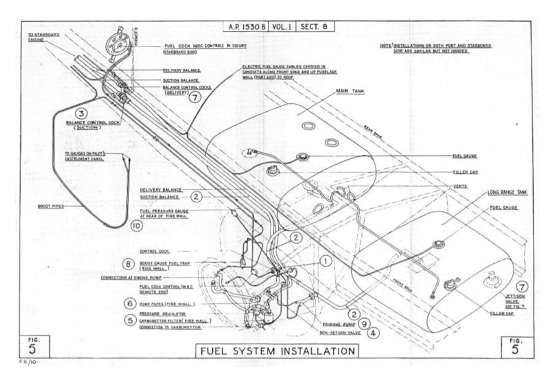

A.P. 1530 B | VOL. I | SECT. 8

FUEL SYSTEM INSTALLATION

FIG. 5

panels on the underside of the mainplanes and bolted to brackets on the spars.

The fuel cocks and the suction and delivery balance cock are actuated by mechanical remote control cables led from the fuel cock control handwheels on the starboard side of the pilot's cockpit. To open or close or switch over the cocks, the control wheels are turned so that the selected settings, engraved on the control handwheels, are opposite the arrow on the indicator plate immediately above.

Each engine has a directly driven dual-type fuel pump for supplying fuel to the carburettor, each pump being fitted with two relief valve springs – one for each valve – set to relieve at a pressure of $3\frac{1}{2}$lb/in^2.

Oil system

Each engine is provided with a separate oil system. Although identical in operation, the port and starboard systems are discrete installations, the only difference being in the run of the pipelines and the mounting of the oil cleaners, which take the inboard positions in each engine nacelle.

The main oil tanks are strapped to cradles on the top forward cross member of each engine mounting structure, while the auxiliary oil tanks are secured by straps immediately outboard of the main oil tanks. Each auxiliary tank is connected by means of a branch on its underside, to the bottom of the corresponding main tanks. A partial oil circulating chamber to assist in the warming up of the oil in cold weather is embodied in each main tank. A Tecalemit oil cleaner and a Serck drum-type oil cooler, which incorporates a relief valve and a bypass unit, is fitted to the oil return pipes between the tank and the engine. The relief valve is set to bypass at 15lb/in². The coolers are mounted across the front of the fireproof bulkhead below the cowling, and the cleaners are mounted vertically below the coolers.

These main tanks, one for each engine, are similar in construction and are interchangeable. They are constructed of aluminium alloy, each tank having a capacity of 11½ gallons of oil, plus 1¾ gallons of air space. In the tank is a partial and normal circulation device which controls the flow of the oil within the tank.

The auxiliary tanks are of cylindrical form and secured, immediately outboard of the main tanks, to the engine mounting structures by straps. Communication with the corresponding main tank is by means of a branch integral with and at the bottom of each auxiliary tank. At the top of each auxiliary tank is a vent from which a pipe is led to join the main tank vent pipe. The tanks are constructed of aluminium alloy, the capacity of each tank being 2½ gallons of oil.

The oil cooler for each engine is strapped to a cradle on the top forward face of the fireproof bulkhead. The cooling air is collected by two ducts extending forward of the engine and is exhausted by a duct to the surface of the nacelle fairing. A relief valve bypasses the oil if the pressure rises above 15lb/in².

The oil cleaner, which is in the return pipe from the carburettor jacket of each engine to the cooler, is supported on the forward face of the fireproof bulkhead, inboard of each engine mounting.

Engine controls

The throttle and mixture control levers for each engine are mounted on a spindle of the engine control box, which is supported on a bracket bolted to a panel on the port side of the pilot's cockpit. A portion of the remote control run between the two engine controls is clamped across the fuselage to the cockpit flooring.

The throttle and mixture levers are

ABOVE The oil tank, oil cooler and system pipework of the port engine are clear to see with the nacelle removed. *(Jarrod Cotter)*

BELOW A diagram illustrating the installation of the oil system. *(Air Ministry)*

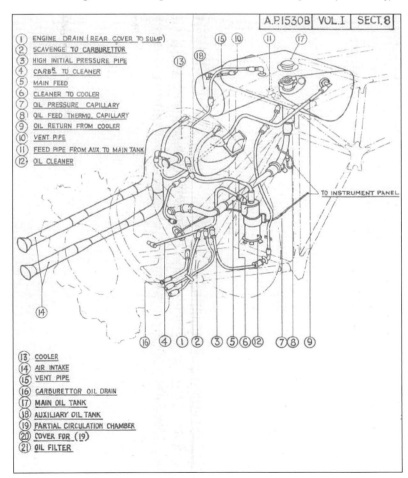

A.P.1530B VOL.I SECT.8

1. ENGINE DRAIN (REAR COVER TO SUMP)
2. SCAVENGE TO CARBURETTOR
3. HIGH INITIAL PRESSURE PIPE
4. CARBR. TO CLEANER
5. MAIN FEED
6. CLEANER TO COOLER
7. OIL PRESSURE CAPILLARY
8. OIL FEED THERMO. CAPILLARY
9. OIL RETURN FROM COOLER
10. VENT PIPE
11. FEED PIPE FROM AUX TO MAIN TANK
12. OIL CLEANER

TO INSTRUMENT PANEL

13. COOLER
14. AIR INTAKE
15. VENT PIPE
16. CARBURETTOR OIL DRAIN
17. MAIN OIL TANK
18. AUXILIARY OIL TANK
19. PARTIAL CIRCULATION CHAMBER
20. COVER FOR (19)
21. OIL FILTER

connected to the layshafts and operating rods in the engine nacelles by torque tubes supported by iolite bearings along the leading edge of the centre mainplane.

Propeller pitch controls

The controls for changing the pitch of the airscrew blades are mounted on a control panel on which can also be found the controls for the air-intake shutters and the carburettor cut-outs. The controls for the airscrews are the bottom pair and are situated below a similar pair fitted with a hinged cover on the same panel. The

control panel is adjacent to the front spar at the rear of the cockpit and is within easy reach of the pilot. The push-pull knobs which operate the airscrew pitch control are coloured red for port and green for starboard. Their operations are push for fine pitch and pull for coarse pitch. Mechanical remote controls, each approximately 9ft 6in long and extending along the centre plane, are used for coupling the push-pull knobs to the control of each airscrew.

Air-intake shutter controls

The carburettors are each fitted with an air-intake shutter, each being separately controlled by a lever. These levers are mounted on the same panel as that employed for the carburettor cut-out and the propeller pitch controls, and are situated at the top of the panel. The levers are coloured red for port and green for starboard and are each connected by mechanical remote controls. Each control is approximately 9ft 6in long and extends along the centre mainplane and terminates at a lever which, in turn, is coupled by means of a pulley-guided cable, to the shutter on the carburettor of each engine. When the levers in the cockpit are at the top, they are in the cold weather position for starting, fine weather conditions and full power etc., but when the levers are at the bottom, they are in the hot air position for warming-up, low air temperature, gliding, damp atmosphere, rain and snow, clouds, etc.

Carburettor cut-out controls

Each engine is fitted with a carburettor cut-out control. These controls are operated by means of the knobs below the hinged covers and are mounted as a pair on the same panel as that used for the air-intake shutter and the propeller pitch controls and are employed for stopping the engines quickly. To do this it is necessary first to close the throttles, switch off the magnetos, and then pull the cut-out control knob and hold it until the engine is stationary. The controls are returned to the normal position by compression springs at the front of the firewall in the nacelles. Mechanical remote controls, each approximately 9ft 0in long and extending along the centre mainplane, are employed for the operation of this control.

Hydraulic system

The hydraulic system operates the flaps, the gun turret and the port and starboard undercarriage retracting mechanisms, each of which is actuated by a jack. Power is supplied to these jacks by fluid under pressure energised by an engine-driven pump or, if that is not working, by a hand pump.

This system comprises a fluid reservoir, an engine-driven pump, a hand pump, a main and a non-return relief valve, a selector valve, a flap control and an undercarriage control valve, a flap jack, two undercarriage operating jacks, two undercarriage locking jacks, three gun and turret operating jacks, a filter and necessary piping and connections.

Pneumatic system

The pneumatic system supplies power for operating the wheel brakes, the fuel jettison valve, the firing unit of the Browning machine gun and the camera gun. From the engine-driven air compressor on the starboard engine, an air pipe is led through the firewall

to the oil reservoir, thence to the oil trap. From the oil trap an air pipe is led along, within the nose of the centre mainplane, to the fuselage, thence to the bottom connection of the air container. The air supply to the wheel brakes, the fuel jettison valves, the Browning machine-gun control and the camera gun control, is taken from the top connection of the air container from which a pipe is led via a charging connection T-piece and the air filter to a three-way connection. From one branch of this installation a pipe is taken, via the minimum pressure cut-out valve, to the fuel

ABOVE Each carburettor is attached to an air-intake shutter, which are each separately controlled and positioned on the undersurface of the engine nacelle. *(Jarrod Cotter)*

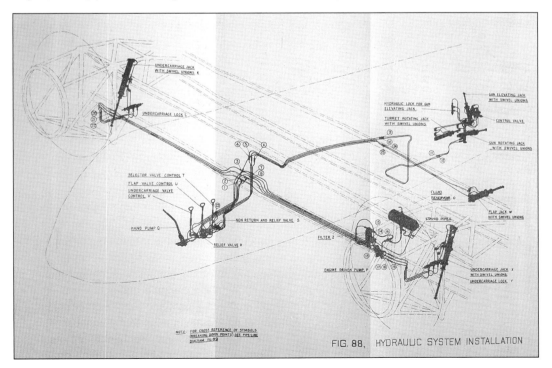

FIG. 88, HYDRAULIC SYSTEM INSTALLATION

LEFT An illustration showing the installation of the hydraulic system which operates the flaps, undercarriage and turret. *(Air Ministry)*

RIGHT A fold-out diagram showing the installation of the Blenheim's pneumatic system. *(Air Ministry)*

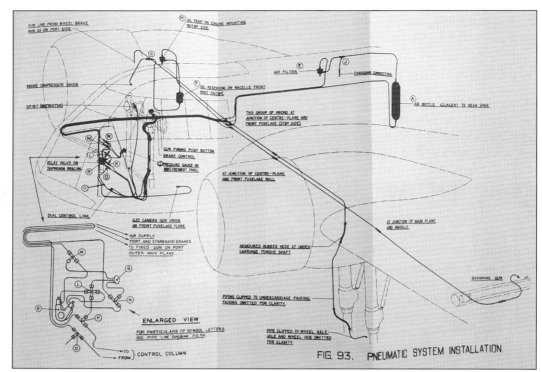

FIG. 93. PNEUMATIC SYSTEM INSTALLATION.

BELOW An illustration showing the installation of the fixed Browning machine gun in the port wing. *(Air Ministry)*

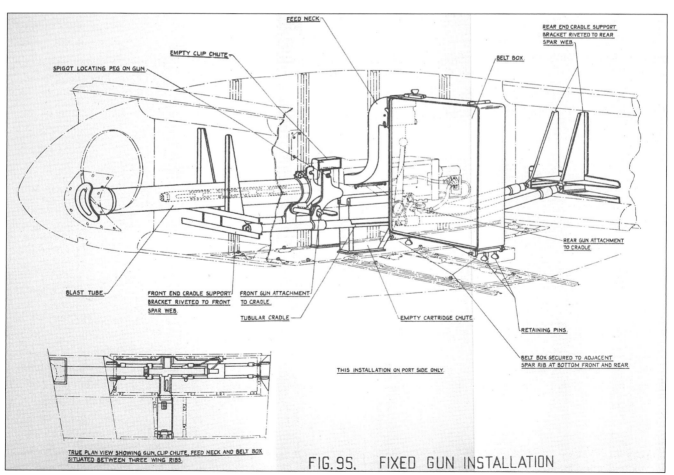

FIG. 95. FIXED GUN INSTALLATION

RIGHT **In the cockpit the pilot has a fold-down ring sight for the fixed machine gun.** *(Jarrod Cotter)*

control valve, thence to the fuel jettison valves. From the remaining branch of the connection a pipe is taken to a second three-way joint. The air supply to the wheel brakes is taken from one branch of this three-way connection, while from the remaining branch an air supply pipe is led, via the gun firing button, to a third three-way connection. From one branch of this a pipe is led forward, then aft along the fuselage starboard side, along the nose of the port portion of the centre mainplane. From the remaining branch of the three-way connection a pipe is led down and aft to the camera-gun control.

Armament

The Blenheim is equipped with a pilot-controlled fixed Browning 0.303in machine gun in the port wing and a Vickers 0.303in machine gun mounted in the gun turret. The fixed gun is located in the port outer mainplane on a detachable non-adjustable tubular cradle. The firing of the gun is pneumatically controlled, a flexible pipe connecting the trigger motor to the pneumatic pipeline. The feed neck extends between the belt box and the gun, and is secured in position by quick-release pins.

When the gun is being installed in the aeroplane it is first mounted on its cradle, which is then placed in the wing. The gun is set to fire parallel to the horizontal datum and to converge at a point 400yd ahead on the gun sight line.

The pilot's gun foresight for the fixed gun is mounted externally on the port side of the nose portion of the fuselage (Mk IV). The aft ring sight is suspended from the top of the pilot's cockpit. Both foresight and aft ring sight are adjustable.

Gun turret

The Bristol gun turret is traversing. The lowering and raising of the gun and the gunner's seat are each effected by a hydraulically operated

jack. Turrets were initially equipped with a Lewis Type K 0.303in machine gun, and later two Brownings. Finnish-built Blenheim turrets were equipped with an L-33/34 machine gun and a Vickers VGO reflector sight.

Bomb loads

Provision is made for the carriage of bombs on two No 2-type EM/EF and four No 1-type EM/EF bomb carriers. The carriers selected for use are

BELOW **The turret of a Finnish-built Blenheim, equipped with an L-33/34 machine gun and a Vickers VGO reflector sight.** *(SA-Kuva)*

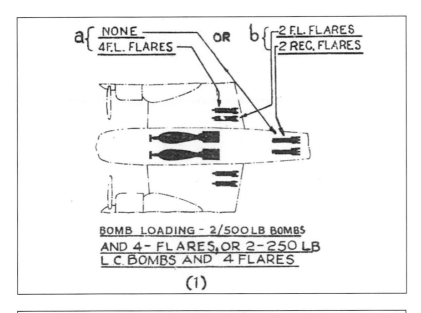

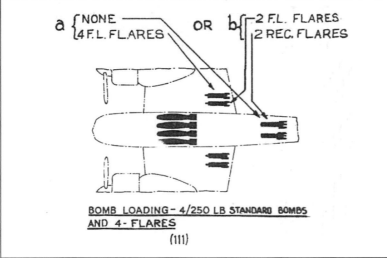

carried in the fuselage bomb compartments below the centre plane front and rear spars. In addition to the above carriers, provision is made for mounting two EN-type light-series carriers on the underside of the fuselage, immediately aft of the bomb compartments. Housing is also provided in the wing roots for four flares, two on each side.

Provision is made for carriage of the following alternative bomb loads:

(i) Two 500lb GP bombs and four flares*
or two 500lb SAP bombs and four flares*
or two 500lb AS bombs and four flares*
or two 250lb LC bombs and four flares*

(ii) Two 250lb Type B bombs and four flares

(iii) Four 250lb GP bombs and four flares*
or four 250lb SAP bombs and four flares*
or four 250lb AS bombs and four flares*

(iv) Eight practice bombs

(v) Six flares

(vi) Two 250lb small-bomb containers and four flares.

* For bomb loadings (i) and (iii), the following flares may be carried as alternatives to the four, stated above, housed in the centre plane roots: two 4in training flares for forced-landing can be carried in the centre plane roots together with two 4.5in reconnaissance flares which can be carried on one of the light-series carriers normally fitted for practice bombs. When no bombs are carried two training flares for forced-landing plus four 4.5in reconnaissance flares can be carried on an external light-series carrier. In addition, provision is made for carrying a 250lb small-bomb container and four flares.

ABOVE AND RIGHT
Three of the various bomb-loading options of the Blenheim.
(Air Ministry)

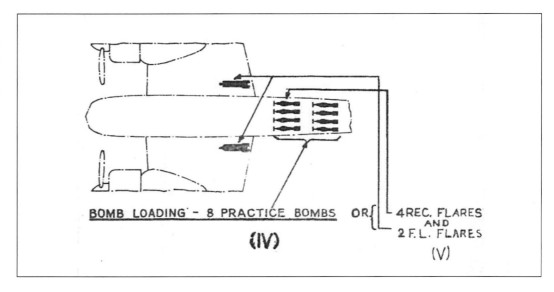

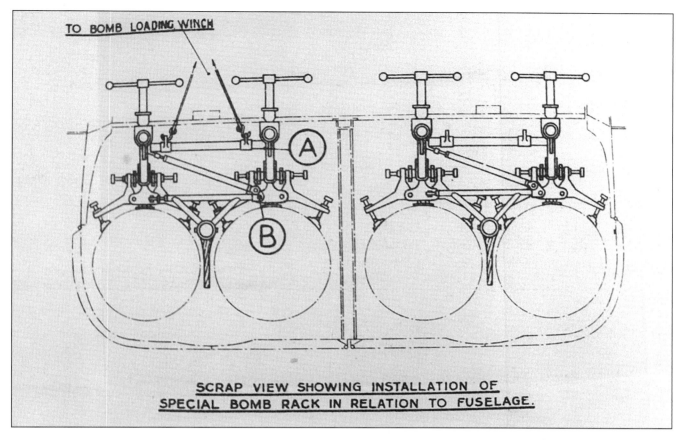

TO BOMB LOADING WINCH

Ⓐ

Ⓑ

SCRAP VIEW SHOWING INSTALLATION OF
SPECIAL BOMB RACK IN RELATION TO FUSELAGE.

The 500lb and 250lb bombs and also the 250lb small-bomb container are carried in the fuselage bomb compartments, the practice bombs being mounted on the light-series carriers secured to the bottom of the fuselage. The bombs are fused and released electrically, and the entire bomb load can be jettisoned by the bomb-aimer or by the pilot.

Oxygen apparatus

Two 750-litre oxygen cylinders are stowed in the rear fuselage on the starboard side, near the rear spar. When the full crew of three is carried, an additional oxygen cylinder is mounted horizontally below the two cylinders initially installed.

ABOVE A diagram illustrating the double bomb carriers in a Blenheim. *(Air Ministry)*

LEFT Light-series bomb racks fitted with dummy practice bombs. *(Jarrod Cotter)*

'It's always a thrilling, fascinating moment when the engines of a restored aircraft burst into life for the first time because then it becomes a living machine, no longer just a collection of dead machinery.'

Graham Warner, former RAF pilot and once owner of Blenheim G-BPIV

Chapter Four

The owner's view

Due to the number of surviving Blenheim airframes, and the few people experienced in restoring them, while the warbird world has numerous owners of airworthy Spitfires, Mustangs, B-25 Mitchells and B-17 Flying Fortresses to draw from, there have only ever been a few owners of the world's only airworthy Bristol Blenheim. Having been involved with the first project to flight and now owner of a Blenheim and the world's only current type-qualified pilot, John Romain shares his passion for this historic aircraft by telling how he flies it.

OPPOSITE John Romain at the controls of L6739, the world's only airworthy Bristol Blenheim and the only complete Blenheim Mk I seen since the Second World War, which is pictured following an early air test on its way back to Duxford, 3 December 2014. *(Jarrod Cotter)*

RIGHT John Romain, the world's only current Blenheim pilot, standing in front of Mk I L6739 outside the ARC hangar at Duxford. *(Jarrod Cotter)*

Walking around the Blenheim you become aware of a number of things. Firstly, it is not small! At least on the outside. It is also a great design. The contours seem to blend into each other, making for a pleasant, well-designed appearance. It also looks purposeful, the engines in particular giving a sense of power and attitude.

The design is pre-war and so there are certain aspects of it that differ from the later twin-engined, mostly American aircraft that the RAF used. Fuel priming for the engine is in the undercarriage bays and not in the cockpit, therefore groundcrew are definitely required in the start process. The brakes are pneumatic-powered, as are most British types, so air pressures are to be maintained by external sources before a start. It is also 12-volt and so before the days of powerful 12-volt batteries, a trolley 'ack' was required for starting. If this was not available you can hard-start the engines with a crank handle stowed in the rear fuselage for this purpose. Today though, we have adequate electrical power, pneumatic pressure and a helpful groundcrew to prime and carry out the 'sucking in' process on the engines.

Climbing aboard

With the external checks done, it is time to get in. This is always achieved by climbing up over the rear fuselage and dropping into the sliding hatch above the pilot's seat. The rear gunner, if carried, goes through a top hatch

RIGHT For crew access to a Blenheim there are footrests and handgrips on the port fuselage sides below the turret area and a non-slip walkway on the port wing. The pilot and bomb-aimer or navigator enters the cockpit and nose area through a sliding hood over the pilot's seat. The gunner or wireless operator enters the rear section/turret area through an inward-opening door on the roof forward of the turret with a short ladder placed below it. Here John Romain climbs aboard Mk I L6739 for a local sortie out of Duxford. *(Jarrod Cotter)*

just in front of the turret, while the navigator follows the pilot through the sliding hatch.

The pilot's seat is comfortable, even having armrests if required! A conventional four-point harness holds you in. Electrical power is switched on from the rear fuselage seat position and a check of the undercarriage lights and general electrical systems follows.

Start-up

With the crew in, it is time to start the engines. Fuel is selected from a fuel selection unit located on the right-hand side of the cockpit. This unit also controls fuel 'suction and balance'. These are used if you were required to run one engine from both left and right fuel tanks or individually as required. Normal operation is for the left tank to supply the left engine and the right tank feeds the right engine. Fuel quantity gauges are above and behind the pilot's head and fuel pressure gauges are located on the rear right-hand panel. The fuel pressure on the engines runs quite low, normally at 3½psi. Due to the head of fuel from the tanks you can see 1½psi register on the gauges as soon as the fuel selector is turned to 'on'.

Brakes are tested, the pneumatic pressure checked at a minimum of 100psi, and then the parking brake is selected. The magneto switches are checked at 'off' and the groundcrew now prime the engines. A cold start will require three full primes, five blades then pulled through on the propellers and a further two shots of prime. A hot start is normally one or two shots of prime only. With the groundcrew now clear, the throttles are set at ½in open and the magnetos switched to 'on'. Once the starter button is pushed, the engines start readily and soon settle at about 600–700rpm. Oil pressure is checked as rising or sitting above 90psi – it normally rises very quickly and so any undue delay needs investigating instantly, which requires a shut-down.

While the engines are warming up the other checks can be made prior to taxi:
- Cowl gills – fully open
- Propeller controls to fine pitch
- Oil pressure minimum 70psi

LEFT A cold start of the Blenheim requires three full primes, five blades then pulled through on the propellers and a further two shots of prime. Here the propellers are being pulled through. (Jarrod Cotter)

- Oil temperature – rising
- Cylinder-head temperature – rising
- Fuel – check quantity, pressure 3½psi and both selected 'on'
- Hydraulic pressure – checked at 750psi
- Carburettor air – cold
- Mixtures – auto rich
- Brake pressure – minimum 100psi
- Vacuum pressure – 4½psi
- Gyros – uncaged
- Avionics – on and tested.

The Blenheim taxis very easily and normal turns can be made without brakes. The rudder is powerful but the engines can also be used to steer the aircraft. Visibility is good to the front and the left but a little restricted to the right due to the cockpit side and the engine.

BELOW Fuel priming for the engines is performed in the undercarriage bays and not in the cockpit, therefore groundcrew are an essential part of the aircraft's start-up. (Jarrod Cotter)

Pre-take-off checks

Once at the threshold the engines can be tested prior to the pre-take-off checks being carried out. However, I normally make most of the pre-take-off checks early, so avoiding the engines being at idle for too long after their checks.

So, trim settings on rudder and elevator are at neutral.

■ Brakes – on – pressure still above 100psi
■ Flaps – check operation and select 'up'
■ Hydraulic selector – pressure checked at 750psi
■ Fuel – on both, pressure at 3½psi
■ Propeller – fine pitch
■ Magnetos – on both
■ Cowl gills – open
■ Controls – full and free
■ Hatches and harnesses – all closed and secure
■ Crew brief – carried out.

With a minimum of 40°C oil temperature, we can now perform the engine power runs. Individually the engines are powered up to 1,850rpm. The oil pressure is checked and then the propeller control is selected into coarse pitch. A drop of 300–400rpm is noted and the propeller control selected back to fine pitch. Warm air is then selected on the carburettor intake and a slight reduction in rpm is noted.

Zero boost is then selected and 2,050rpm noted. Magnetos are checked and oil temperature and pressure checked as being in the correct range. Finally the throttle is gradually closed and an idle rpm of 550–650 is noted. With both engines checked the final pre-take-off checks are carried out and we are ready to go.

Airborne

The aircraft accelerates freely and at 80–90mph the tail is lifted to enable the airspeed to increase to 105mph before lift-off. If one engine should fail at this speed, or above, then the aircraft can still fly on one engine – below 105mph you would have to put it down again.

Once airborne the undercarriage is selected 'up' and the aircraft accelerated to 120mph. The controls feel good on this aircraft and as the speed increases I start to reduce the power and then select the propellers into 'coarse'. This is like changing gear on a car; the rpm drops by about 400rpm and the aircraft starts to accelerate to a normal course speed of about 195mph.

Once settled I do the after-take-off checks:

■ Undercarriage up – indicator lights out
■ Hydraulics – selected to 'off' or 'turret' if that is to be used
■ Flaps – up, if used
■ Carb air – warm air
■ Temperatures and pressures – all in range
■ Mixtures – auto lean.

General handling

General handling of the aircraft is very good. It rolls very easily and is a pleasant flying machine. A keen eye is always present on the engines, though. They are rare, need careful handling and will let you know if they are not happy!

If there is anyone in the rear fuselage they can use the turret. It is hydraulically operated and not only turns but the gunner rises and lowers with the gun. To use it now is great fun, but I would imagine in wartime with a Messerschmitt Bf 109 on your tail it was not fun at all.

Display routine

A typical display profile is fairly easily flown. A mixture of flybys and wingovers with speed trading for height and vice versa works well. The display is normally flown at zero boost, in coarse pitch and a minimum of 105mph is used in the wingovers. The initial run-in is about 220mph and this works well in achieving a good climb for the wingovers.

The view from the cockpit is very good in the air. The Mk I has a lot of frontal glass and so you can see all about you and even down past the nose to the ground.

Next to the pilot, the navigator has the choice of two seats once airborne. A bomb-aiming seat is located forward of the normal seat. This is right up in the nose and gives a great view – especially down of course.

Landing

Back to the airfield and it's time to land. Mixtures go to auto rich before descending and the hydraulics are selected from 'turret' to 'undercarriage/flaps'. A run and break is normal and this puts the aircraft at 120mph downwind.

Throttles are set at -4lb boost initially and the propellers are selected to fine pitch. Halfway downwind, the undercarriage is selected 'down' and the brake pressure is checked. In addition the following checks finish the landing checks.

- Brakes – off, pressure minimum 100psi
- Undercarriage – down, two greens
- Mixture – rich
- Fuel – on, tanks' quantity checked and pressure 3½psi
- Propellers – fine pitch
- Hydraulics – 750psi
- Carb air – cold
- Flaps – as required, but full flaps on finals
- Temperatures and pressure – all good
- Hatches and harnesses – secure.

A speed of 105mph is maintained, at half flap until a landing is confirmed. Then full flap and 85mph can be used on short finals.

The Blenheim three-points very well and soon settles down on the runway. Directional control is good and little braking is required unless you wish to slow down quicker than normal.

The gills are selected to fully open at the end of the landing run to keep the cylinders cool. Flaps are selected 'up' and the taxi completed to parking.

To cool the engines and scavenge the engine oil it is normal to let the engine idle for about two minutes. Then the idle cut-offs are pulled and silence arrives! Switches all go off and out we get.

It is a very rare and beautiful aircraft. It flies very well and is a real testament to the designers of the early 1930s. Simply fantastic!

BELOW General handling of the Blenheim Mk I is very good. It rolls easily and is a pleasant flying machine which allows the pilot great visibility. However, a keen eye is always needed to watch over the performance of the Bristol Mercury engines, as they are rare and need careful handling.
(Jarrod Cotter)

'You cannot compare the Mosquito and the Blenheim. They were two quite different aircraft, but I will always retain a great fondness for the Blenheim, which gave me my first taste of action.'

Air Marshal Sir Ivor Broom
KCB CBE DSO DFC** AFC,
former Blenheim and Mosquito pilot

Chapter Five

The crew's view

In the previous chapter John Romain described how he flies the world's only airworthy Bristol Blenheim. However, while this now-unique airworthy machine is flown with the utmost of care and respect due to its huge historical importance, flying Blenheims in the hostile environment it was designed for called for an altogether different mindset when it came to flying operations. Here we offer a taste of the wartime instructions that were issued to the 'Blenheim Boys' with stylised text based on the information from AP1530A *Pilot's Notes*.

OPPOSITE The pilot and navigator of a 139 Squadron Bristol Blenheim Mk IV are seen in early war period flying clothing while in the cockpit of their aircraft in France during 1940. *(Air Ministry)*

101

Preliminaries

On entering the cockpit the pilot must ensure that the hydraulic selector lever is down and also that the undercarriage operating lever is down. He should then switch on the undercarriage indicator lamps and check that the undercarriage is locked, which is indicated by green lights. Next, the contents of the fuel tanks should be checked. He must then ensure the flying controls all move freely, set the carburettor air intake heat controls to cold and set the cowling gills fully open. The final preliminary operation is to set the propeller controls to fine pitch.

Engine start and warm-up

The fuel cock control wheels should be set as required. If the aircraft is loaded for long-range flight, the run-up and take-off must be made with the fuel supply from the outer tanks, with the others turned off.

Groundcrew should then be instructed to prime the engines and switch on the starting magnetos. Six to eight full pumps are required to prime a cold engine, but only two or three are needed if the engines are still hot.

Next, the pilot needs to set the throttle levers approximately ½in forward on the quadrant. The levers should not be set further open than this otherwise fuel will be pumped into the air intake, causing a risk of fire.

Having called 'clear prop' and getting a response from the groundcrew to ensure all personnel are clear of the propellers, the main magneto switches should be turned on. Then the starter button of each engine should be pressed in turn, but for no longer than ten seconds continuously. The left hand should be kept on the throttle lever during the start and if the engine 'spits back' through the carburettor, the throttle lever should be pulled right back and then slowly opened to give a fast tick-over. The engines should be warmed up at a fast tick-over until the oil temperatures are at least 5°C and the cylinder temperatures around 100°C.

Engine tests

Throttles should not be opened fully for more than a few seconds and only long enough to make the necessary checks. During the warm-up period, the pilot should instruct the groundcrew to switch off the starting magnetos. He should then test the operation of the hydraulic pump by selecting the flaps down and then returning them to up. During running-up, each engine should be checked for static rpm at $+5lb/in^2$ boost (2,300–2,400) then at $+9lb/in^2$ boost (2,500–2,600).

Except immediately before take-off, the change-over to high boost must only be made with the throttle in the take-off position. The time during which the engine is run at $+9lb/in^2$ boost pressure on the ground must not exceed two seconds. While the boost control is set in the high boost position, any subsequent throttling down must be made with no pause between full throttle and slow running, but the high boost control lever should be moved to the 'up' position *before* throttling back.

BELOW A Finnish crew prepare to climb into their Blenheim. Note the uniform they are wearing. *(SU-Kuva)*

The oil pressure may be well over 100lb/in^2 while the oil temperature is low. However, it will drop to a normal reading of 80lb/in^2 when the temperature returns to normal.

Testing of the magnetos and spark plugs should be done at +5lb/in^2 of boost and full throttle – *not* at +9lb/in^2 boost. The drop in rpm should not exceed around 100. If the engine misfires or runs roughly, or the rpm drop exceeds 100, the aircraft must not be flown.

Taxying out

For braking during taxying, a minimum pressure of 100lb/in^2 must be in the air cylinder. The pilot must ensure that the safely pins are removed from the radius rods of each undercarriage unit.

After releasing the parking brake, the engines can be opened up to move off. Taxying is normal and changes of direction should be made by

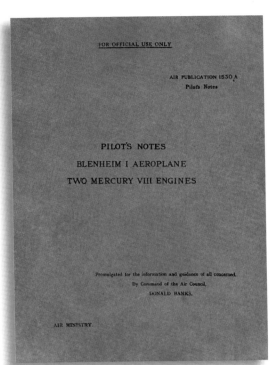

LEFT The cover of AP1530A, *Pilot's Notes* for the Blenheim Mk I. *(Air Ministry)*

BELOW A trio of Blenheim Mk Is silhouetted against an atmospheric skyscape. *(Air Ministry)*

The following series of photographs shows the main procedures and controls used to start the engines of Blenheim I L6739. On top of the usual safety requirements to make sure the aircraft is in good order to fly, due to the rarity of the Blenheim and its engines, the procedure can take some time in order to check and double-check that everything is running well. If you see the crew enter L6739 prior to it flying at an air show it can be fascinating to watch all that's involved in the process from both the aircrew and groundcrew. These photographs, specially posed to show readers of this Haynes Manual the Blenheim's start-up procedure, were taken by George Romain.

1 Electrical power is switched on with the master switch from the rear fuselage seat position, and a check of the undercarriage lights and general electrical systems follows.

2 and 3 The fuel cock controls should be selected from off to on.

4 Brakes are tested, the pneumatic pressure checked at a minimum of 100psi, and then the parking brake is selected.

5 and 6 The pilot checks that the magneto switches are off, and then the groundcrew prime the engines from inside the wheel bays. A cold start will require three full primes, five blades then pulled through on the propellers, and a further two shots of prime.

7 With the groundcrew clear, the throttles are set at ½in open.

8 Then the magnetos are switched on.

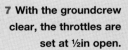

9 The hinged cover over the starter buttons is raised, then the buttons are pushed and the engines start readily.

10 Prior to taxying, the pilot checks that the oil pressure is rising or sitting above 90psi. It normally rises very quickly and so any undue delay needs investigating, which will require a shut-down. Checks are also made that the oil temperature is rising. *(All George Romain)*

Take-off

After completion of the above checks, the crew should search the sky for approaching aircraft, then turn into wind and take off without delay. Both throttles should be opened together, and should be done so in only two or three seconds. With the Blenheim loaded to its long-range 14,500lb load, the take-off run is about 400yd in still air, at maximum rpm and +9lb/in^2 boost.

During the take-off run there is a slight tendency for the Blenheim to swing to the right, which should be corrected by the use of the rudder. As speed builds, the tail should be raised almost to flying position with the nose held at a constant attitude allowing the aircraft to rotate by itself with the increase in speed and lift.

After take-off

As soon as the Blenheim has completely left the ground, pause for no more than about five seconds to ensure ample flying speed has been achieved. Once the pilot is sure the aircraft will not touch the ground again, the pilot's first immediate action after take-off should be to raise the undercarriage. The aircraft should then be maintained in almost level flight to gather speed as quickly as possible.

When the airspeed indicator is reading 120mph, the propeller pitch should be changed to coarse. A gentle climb should then be maintained until the speed rises to 150mph indicated. If the take-off has been made at +9lb/in^2 boost, the high boost lever must now be moved up to give +5lb/in^2 boost – and this must be done before throttling back to the rated position. If flaps have been used for the take-off, once a safe height of 300–400ft is reached, they can be raised.

Once the above actions have been made, the following can be carried out at leisure, though without undue delay. Oil pressures must be checked, the oil and cylinder temperatures should also be checked and the cowling gills need to be adjusted as required. The hydraulic selector must then be moved to the fully up position to allow the gun turret to be operated.

means of the rudder and engines. During lengthy taxying, checks must be made regularly to ensure that the cylinder temperatures do not rise too high and that the brake pressure is good.

If the take-off run is delayed, then each engine should be cleared in turn by running them up at zero boost against the brakes. Engines should not tick over for more than two or three minutes without being cleared.

On reaching the take-off position, the pilot should bring his Blenheim to a halt across-wind facing the airfield circuit so that any approaching aircraft can be seen. He should then commence the following drill of vital actions, some of which may have already been made before or during the taxi-out, but must be checked in the correct sequence before *every* take-off:

- Hydraulic selector – down
- Tabs – neutral
- Mixture control – normal (fully back)
- Pitch – fine (pushed in to rear)
- Gills – one-third open for long-range load (14,500lb)
- Gills – fully closed for normal load (12,500lb)
- Flaps – use of flaps should be avoided if possible for take-off, but in the case of operating at a heavy load (14,500lb) or for a short run they should be lowered to 15°
- Boost control – down for long-range load, +9lb/in^2
- Boost control – up for normal load, +5lb/in^2.

However, if during the sortie there is no possibility of the turret needing to be operated, the selector lever can be placed in neutral. Then the engine should be throttled back and the mixture control adjusted as required.

Climbing

The aeroplane may be climbed in coarse pitch at full throttle ($+5\text{lb/in}^2$ boost) if necessary, but that is uneconomical. Engine temperatures must be monitored and if they approach their limiting figures, which are only allowed for a comparatively short duration of a climb, the cowling gills should be opened a little. The limits are 80°C for the oil temperature and 210°C (30-minute limit) for the cylinder-head temperature. The best climbing speed at full throttle is about 150mph up to 10,000ft. It should then be reduced uniformly to 140mph at 15,000ft and 130mph at 20,000ft. The engines should normally be run at the lowest speed necessary for the occasion.

Cruising

The Blenheim has a good reserve of power and will fly with its engines throttled down to less than 1,600rpm, which will economise fuel and reduce maintenance.

LEFT **The wireless operator/air gunner of a 404 Squadron RCAF Bolingbroke demonstrates the method of climbing aboard the aircraft.** *(404 Squadron RCAF)*

The absolute limit of engine speed in level flight is 2,750rpm at $+5\text{lb/in}^2$ boost (for not more than five minutes). Maximum cruising rpm should only be exceeded in an emergency and with 100-octane fuel at $+9\text{lb/in}^2$ boost, an increase of approximately 20mph can be expected at altitudes below 9,000ft, but no increase of boost pressure or top speed is obtainable above 14,000ft with the use of 100-octane fuel.

BELOW **The Commanding Officer of 211 Squadron, Squadron Leader J.R. Gordon-Finlayson, and his wireless operator/air gunner, Pilot Officer A.C. Geary, photographed in a Blenheim Mk I at Menidi-Tatoi, Greece, after returning from Corfu on 24 November 1941. His aircraft was hit by anti-aircraft fire during a bombing raid on Valona, Albania, and unable to make it back to Menidi, he force-landed on a beach on Corfu, where he and his crew were toasted before returning to the mainland on a fishing boat to rejoin their unit.** *(Air Ministry)*

The limits for continuous cruising with the mixture control set to normal are 2,400rpm and +3½lb boost. With the mixture control set to weak the limits are 2,400rpm and +1½lb boost. Those settings are suitable for long-distance cruising at high speed, although the aircraft will only be able to fly to considerably less than maximum range as the fuel economy is poor.

To achieve an economical cruise, the lowest fuel consumption can be obtained by using the mixture control in the weak setting and throttling back to fly at the lowest speed at which the Blenheim will fly with the engines running smoothly. The best economy of miles per gallon can be obtained by flying at a slightly higher speed than the lowest speed mentioned earlier.

At 15,000ft the greatest range is obtained at a speed of 110mph ASI. Such a low speed as this is impracticable in disturbed air, so at low altitudes the best speed for achieving an extended range is about 130mph ASI. These speeds are useful if fuel is running short.

Other considerations that need to be taken into account during the cruise are that the cowling gills must be fully closed for economical cruising and the oil and cylinder temperate limits must never be exceeded. Also, the engines should be run at the same speed by eliminating 'heterodyne beat' [a difference]. The boost gauges give a good guide, but the rpm indicators are not accurate enough for this purpose. Finally, always use the mixture controls when cruising steadily for any length of time.

General flying

The Blenheim's controls are very positive, effective and well harmonised, almost ideally for this type of aircraft. The elevator becomes very heavy in a steep turn, which is a good feature because it indicates to the pilot that he is increasing the stresses on the structure. The rudder is quite heavy and is amply effective, though it is not used in normal flying.

Directional stability is exceptionally good, although stability in pitch and roll is about

RAF pilot's wings brevet.

RCAF navigator's brevet.

RCAF bomb aimer's brevet.

RCAF wireless operator/air gunner's brevet.

neutral. This means that the Blenheim is very steady in straight and level flight, but will not usually maintain a straight and level course for more than a few seconds 'hands off'. It will very slowly drop or raise the nose and roll into a turn.

The Blenheim is turned by aileron and elevator control. The slight amount of yaw required is obtained automatically owing to the fact that any tendency to sideslip is converted into steady yaw by the effective fin area. The correct incidence corresponding to the angle of bank will be obtained exactly if the nose is kept on the horizon by elevator control, while the bank is kept constant by the ailerons. Rudder control is not required. This eliminates the need for careful co-ordination of hand and foot, and is particularly valuable in flying by instruments.

If the maximum angle of bank for a sustained turn at a particular speed is exceeded for more than a few seconds, stalling incidence will be reached. This would require great force on the elevator control, unless the aircraft is trimmed tail-heavy. The tab trimmer must not be used in this way, therefore steep turns at low speed must not be done.

The following actions will all result in a nose-down attitude and require a change of trim: putting the flaps down; retracting the undercarriage; opening the cowling gills; changing the propeller pitch to fine; and closing the throttles.

The rudder trimming tab is a fine adjustment, though it is also required in case of an engine failure. It can be used to correct any tendency to yaw during flight, and also to trim if the aircraft is flying left or right wing low.

The elevator trimming tab must be used frequently during straight flying to compensate for any change of trim due to the variation of throttle settings. However, it must not be used for manoeuvring, as great stresses can be put on the airframe. It should also not be used for recovery from a dive except as a last resort in an emergency, and even then should be used with the greatest care. The control for the tab should be set partly back for landing, not because it makes the elevator more effective, but because it makes it lighter when flattening out to land.

Flying at slow speeds down to the stall should be practised at a safe height, so that

ABOVE A bomb-aimer takes his position behind a Mk IXA course-setting bombsight in the nose of a 139 Squadron Blenheim Mk IV at Plivot, France, in about April 1940. *(Air Ministry)*

the pilot will become familiar with the feel of the controls. Feet should be put on the rudder pedals at low speed, as it may be required if the aircraft stalls.

Approach and landing

The landing should always be made with flaps fully down, as these reduce the stalling speed and the 'float' and help to stop the run on the ground, especially if there is much wind. High speed may be maintained until the aeroplane nears the aerodrome. A convenient method is to throttle down 'to the hooter', that is, throttle back as far as possible without sounding the undercarriage hooter.

Any non-vital preparations for landing should now be made, such as closing the cowling gills and caging the directional gyro. Then throttle right back, raise the nose and climb to reduce speed. As the speed drops below 150mph ASI, carry out the drill of vital actions for landing, and then enter the circuit at not more than 120mph.

A convenient catchphrase for the drill of vital actions for landing is 'HUP and Flaps'. That is:

H – Hydraulic selector down (push hard to ensure that it is down)

U – Undercarriage down (watch the indicators)

P – Pitch to fine (watch the propellers)

and Flaps – Down (this should actually be delayed until the end of the circuit)

The above drill (except lowering the flaps) should be carried out without pause. The undercarriage indicator studs should be watched to the end and, as the green indicator lights can be difficult to see in daylight, they should be carefully observed to check that the undercarriage units are locked down.

Complete the circuit, slightly beyond gliding distance on the leeward side, turn towards the aerodrome at 1,000ft, lower the flaps fully at 100mph ASI (watch the flap indicator) and approach in level flight slightly across-wind. When almost within gliding distance, throttle back enough to keep the Blenheim gliding straight towards the edge of the aerodrome just beyond the gliding distance all the way down, and turn into wind for the final straight approach. Regulate the glidepath by use of throttles and maintain a constant speed of 75–80mph ASI. Trim slightly tail-heavy with the elevator tabs (this is not essential, but assists landing).

Flatten out smoothly with the engines running at this speed and then close the throttles fully and hold the aeroplane just clear of the ground, easing the control column steadily back until it is fully and firmly back, when the aeroplane will make smooth contact with the ground, all three wheels together.

General remarks on landing

Hold the control column firmly back to prevent the elevators flapping, and, if wheel brakes are used, to help keep the tail on the ground. Keep straight with the rudder, and do not use the brakes unnecessarily. Apply them smoothly and, if the tail lifts, release them and try again.

Do not swing until nearly all speed is lost, as it is bad for the tyres. It may be useful in an emergency, however, and a sharp swing can be made without any tendency to capsize.

After touching down, the flaps control *is not* to be moved until after the aeroplane has come to rest. This is because of the possibility of inadvertent operation of the undercarriage control instead of the flaps control. After coming to rest, look down at the flaps control and raise the flaps. Watch the indicator.

It is important to land tail-down (that is, three-point), with the control column fully back. If held off reasonably close to the ground, the aeroplane will not land appreciably tail-first and even if the tailwheel does make smooth contact with the ground before the main wheels, there is no strain on it. In fact less strain is induced than if the aeroplane comes down wheels-first and then drops its tail, which results in severe bouncing of the tail. After three-point landing and with full use of the brakes, the pilot can be certain of stopping the aeroplane within about 300yd, but if a main-wheel landing is made the run will be of definite length, and use of the brakes is dangerous until the tailwheel is on the ground.

Always make a mental note of the point on the aerodrome short of which the landing (tailwheel down) must be made. If the landing is not made before this point (a touch of the wheels is not a landing), the throttles must be opened fully and another circuit made – if in doubt go round again.

In case of an unsuccessful attempt to land, the aeroplane will climb satisfactorily with the flaps and undercarriage down, but:

(i) Raise the undercarriage immediately.

(ii) Do not raise the flaps until a safe height of about 500ft is reached. Put the nose down slightly and increase the speed to about 100mph ASI, then raise the flaps. Flaps may be raised a little at a time if the handle is 'levered up' just above the neutral position.

(iii) Mislanding should be avoided, as failure of one engine during the take-off with flaps down would necessitate the immediate closing of throttles and landing, whatever the state of the ground ahead.

BLENHEIM PARACHUTE DRILL

Immediately prior to the 'Abandon Aircraft' order being given, the captain is to ensure that the undercarriage wheels are retracted and the engines switched off. On receipt of the 'Abandon Aircraft' signal from the captain, the crew is to abandon the Blenheim as follows:

(i) The wireless operator is to abandon the aircraft by way of the camera aperture hatch, marked PARACHUTE EXIT, climbing down feet first and facing starboard.

(ii) The navigator is to abandon the aircraft by way of the forward bottom hatch, marked PARACHUTE EXIT, climbing down feet first and facing forward.

(iii) When the captain is satisfied that all the crew have left the Blenheim, he is to leave by the forward bottom hatch, climbing out head first so that his back is towards the nose of the aircraft as he goes through the hatch. If for any reason he is unable to leave by this exit, he is to abandon the aircraft by sliding back the cockpit roof and climbing out head first through the opening on to the *starboard* wing so that he faces rearwards; he should at no time raise his body into the airstream or attempt to step out on to the wing.

It is dangerous to use top exits or other exits not marked PARACHUTE EXIT as such, with the exception of the pilot's cockpit hood opening, though this must not be used unless it is impossible to leave by the forward bottom hatch.

BELOW Aircrew of 101 Squadron carry out ground parachute drill training from a Blenheim IV. This shows the pilot's method of exiting via the bottom front hatch, leaving the aircraft head first and facing rearwards so that his back is towards the nose. *(101 Squadron Archives)*

FOR VALOUR IN BLENHEIMS

Of the 32 air Victoria Crosses awarded for actions during the Second World War, three went to Blenheim pilots, two of which were made posthumously. Each was given to a pilot flying one of the three different marks, and each from one of the three main theatres of war. Squadron Leader Arthur Scarf VC was awarded his posthumously for actions flying a Blenheim Mk I in the Far East. Air Commodore Sir Hughie Edwards VC KCMG CB DSO DFC OBE earned his for actions while flying a Blenheim IV in northern Europe. Finally, Wing Commander Hugh Malcolm VC was awarded his medal posthumously for actions flying a Blenheim Mk V in the Middle East.

1 Britain's supreme award for gallantry, the Victoria Cross. Of the 32 air VCs awarded for actions during the Second World War, three went to Blenheim pilots. *(Jarrod Cotter)*

2 Squadron Leader Arthur Scarf VC was given his Victoria Cross posthumously for actions flying a Blenheim Mk I in the Far East on 9 December 1941. *(Crown Copyright)*

3 Wing Commander Hughie Edwards, pictured with his wife and mother-in-law after his Victoria Cross investiture at Buckingham Palace in February 1942. *(AWM)*

4 Wing Commander Hugh Malcolm VC, who was awarded a posthumous VC for his actions while flying Blenheim Mk V BA875/W of 18 Squadron on 4 December 1942. *(Crown Copyright)*

5 Bristol Blenheim Mk I L1134/PT-F of 62 Squadron, which is believed to be the aircraft flown by Arthur Scarf on 9 December 1941 when his actions led to the presentation of a posthumous Victoria Cross. *(© Andy Hay/Flyingart)*

6 Bristol Blenheim Mk IV V6028/GB-D of 105 Squadron, which was being flown by Hughie Edwards on 4 July 1941 when his actions for leading an attack on Bremen led to the award of his Victoria Cross. *(© Andy Hay/Flyingart)*

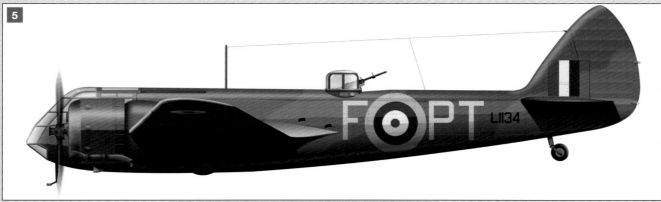

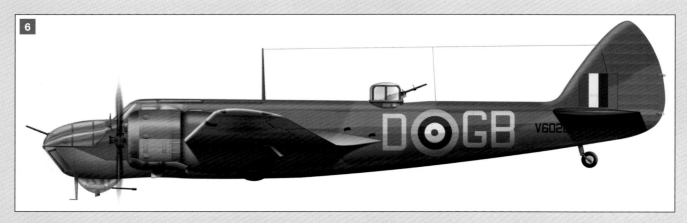

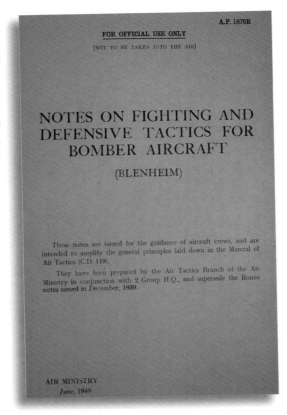

RIGHT The cover of Air Publication 1870B, *Notes on Fighting and Defensive Tactics for Bomber Aircraft (Blenheim),* **dated June 1940.** *(Air Ministry)*

A.P. 1870B

FOR OFFICIAL USE ONLY

(NOT TO BE TAKEN INTO THE AIR)

NOTES ON FIGHTING AND DEFENSIVE TACTICS FOR BOMBER AIRCRAFT

(BLENHEIM)

These notes are issued for the guidance of aircraft crews, and are intended to amplify the general principles laid down in the Manual of Air Tactics (C.D. 119).

They have been prepared by the Air Tactics Branch of the Air Ministry in conjunction with 2 Group H.Q., and supersede the Roneo notes issued in December, 1939.

AIR MINISTRY
June, 1940

The following information is drawn from Air Publication 1870B, *Notes on Fighting and Defensive Tactics for Bomber Aircraft (Blenheim)*, published in June 1940.

Introduction

The tactics described below are based on trials at AFDU between Blenheims and fighters, and on the experience so far gained of German fighter tactics.

Attack by fighters is most dangerous when they can simultaneously engage the maximum number of bombers. The disposition of bomber aircraft and their manoeuvre in formation should therefore aim at:

(a) Presenting a limited front on which the fighters can attack.

(b) Providing supporting firepower on that front.

(c) Giving the fighters a difficult deflection shot.

The approach phase

During this phase the bombers must change from cruising to defensive formation. Tight sections in close 'vic' and 'boxes' are the most suitable dispositions to combine supporting firepower with a limited front for fighters. As a result of recent changes in the defensive armament of Blenheims, the box formation is now considered the most effective formation.

The box formation of six is highly manoeuvrable. The rear three aircraft should take up a position about 50ft below the front three, and about one and a half to two lengths behind, thus eliminating blind spots as far as possible. If the attack develops from the beam and above, the formation should be stepped down slightly towards the attacking fighters; i.e. if the attack is from the port beam, and above, the aeroplane flying on the starboard of the leader should be stepped up and the one on the port of the leader stepped down. If the attack is from the beam and below, the formation should be stepped in the reverse direction; i.e. the aeroplane flying on the port of the leader should be stepped up and the one on the starboard of the leader stepped down. It is quite easy for the aircraft to change height, and there is no risk of inexperienced pilots losing formation. The stepping up and down combined with turns of quite a gentle character should enable six Blenheims to concentrate their fire on the fighters.

Formations of more than nine aircraft become unwieldy or lack cohesion, while individual aircraft and sub-formations may be deprived of the desirable freedom of manoeuvre within the formation. If, therefore, it is desired that operations should be stronger than nine aircraft, two or more formations should operate in company, each formation being free to take independent action and deliver its own attack.

The attack

Fighter aircraft attempt to begin their approach from a position abeam of the bomber formation, though this of course is dependent on the direction in which the sighting first takes place, and the position of the sun and clouds. The fighter formation leader decides on the type of attack to be made while still some distance from the bomber. The difficulty with which the fighter formation leader is faced, is to assess the depth and frontage occupied by the bomber formation, and thus to decide on the maximum number of fighter aircraft that can be deployed against the bombers simultaneously. For example, should a decision be made to attack in squadron strength, and, on arrival in position to open fire, the leader finds that the frontage occupied by the bomber formation is insufficient to accommodate such an attack, then some of his firepower is wasted.

If the change to defensive formation is made shortly before fighters come within the range at which the bombers would normally open fire, the reduction of front may disorganise a mass fighter formation since the wing fighters might be left without a target and so they may tend to collide with adjacent fighters if they attempt to close in.

The attacks developed by Fighter Command for fixed-gun fighters fall into two main classes: those which are delivered from flat astern of the target, and those in which the attack is delivered from astern from a position either higher or lower than the target. In the first few weeks of the war German fighters also attacked from the astern position, varying from slightly below to slightly above the bombers' level.

As a result of the effective counter-fire from the bombers, however, the Me 109 and Me 110 have more recently attacked from the beam, a method of attack which had previously been considered impracticable in view of the very large deflection allowances required.

It is considered that the fire of an eight-gun fighter will not begin to be effective until the range is less than 400 yards. The fire of a four-gun fighter, such as a Messerschmitt 109, will usually be ineffective up to even closer ranges, except in cases where cannon are fitted when the effective range is increased to 600–800 yards.

Although it is important that fire should be opened by the bomber before the fighter opens fire, this policy must be interpreted with intelligence, and fire should not be opened at long ranges; the general policy being to give a sighting burst at 600 yards, and then commence the main volume of fire at 400 yards. Should the fighter stand-off at 800 yards using cannon fire, bombers must not reply by 'blazing away' their limited supply of ammunition. Cannon fire at this range has been found to be completely ineffective. When fighters press home attacks to close ranges, bombers should always endeavour to open fire first in order to disturb the fighters' aim, and possibly destroy them before they can get in a decisive burst.

The manoeuvres of bombers during the attack should be designed:

(a) to induce inaccuracies of aim of the fighters;
(b) to defeat the particular type of attack adopted by the fighters;
(c) when fighters attack in mass, to distract the attention of fighter pilots from their sights by causing them to manoeuvre their aircraft to avoid collision with other fighters.

These manoeuvres should be timed to begin at the moment before the fighter opens fire so that he must realign his sights, during which period defensive fire from the bomber formation can be brought to bear.

Defensive manoeuvres

General considerations

Successful defence against fighters is dependent both upon firepower and on manoeuvre, and the correct timing of these gives the bombers their best chance of success.

The object of manoeuvre is to throw off the aim of the fighters while enabling the bombers to fire. It may be achieved by the changes of course, speed and relative position described hereafter.

The defensive manoeuvres contained in this chapter have been proven in practice to increase the difficulties of fighters when attacking a bomber formation. It is the responsibility of the formation leader to decide which to adopt, as a result of information passed to him by the controller, who will normally be an experienced air gunner or a gunnery officer stationed in the aircraft of the formation leader.

Corkscrewing

When an aircraft flies in a spiral path of, from 4° to 6° from the line of flight, it is said to corkscrew. Corkscrewing gives the fighter a difficult target, as deflection is continually changing.

Undulating

Undulating is an up and down 'switchback' motion which can be made as a section manoeuvre, or by aircraft individually in the section. It should not unduly disturb the air gunners' aim, but will compel the fighter continually to re-sight.

Turning

Turning in formation, before fighters open fire, will throw off the fighters' aim and may enable more rear guns to be brought to bear, if fighters were previously utilising blind spots.

Countermeasures against fixed-gun beam attacks

In recent actions fought between bomber aircraft and enemy fighters there have been instances of the enemy delivering beam attacks. Trials undertaken at the AFDU have confirmed previous experience that such attacks only permit snap-shooting by the fighters, and can be effectively countered by manoeuvres designed to put the attacker on the wrong foot, and to bring the defensive armament of the bombers into play. It is apparent that the length of time in which 'possible hits' would be obtained by this form of attack is in tenths of seconds only. This is with an eight-gun fighter; with the enemy four-gun or cannon fighter, the concentration of fire would be less.

Where beam attack has been experienced, relatively very few hits have been obtained on our aircraft. Generally, therefore, the results of practical experience and of trials coincide. There is, however, the danger of enfilade of the bomber formation, but this can be met by altering the relative positions of the aircraft in the formation.

There is clear evidence to show that the enemy has been forced to resort to these beam attacks, of low tactical value, when our formation tactics and the powerful defensive armament of our bombers have made it hazardous for him to attempt more effective attacks from directly astern.

During AFDU trials the under-mentioned general conclusions were reached concerning the best measures to counter enemy beam attacks. These have now been proved by practical experience.

Beam attack delivered after an approach from ahead

The best counter to this attack is to turn-in towards the fighter, so as to misplace the fighter, and to shorten the closing time between the two aircraft. The turn should be commenced a short time before it appears that the fighter must either deliver an attack, or break away. The point in time is one that can best be judged after some experience, and this manoeuvre should be practised in affiliation exercises.

The 'turn-away' from a beam attack which starts from a position ahead of the formation has little to recommend it as a counter-measure. To be effective it must be a turn of 45 to 50°, and therefore it is liable to upset the cohesion of the formation. Even then it is not certain that the rear guns of the bombers will be able to be brought to bear on the fighters. Nevertheless, it may, on occasion, be preferable to accept these disadvantages inherent in the 'turn-away' in order to get back on the track of the bomber's objective.

Beam attack after an approach from astern

Here again the best countermeasure is the 'turn-in'. The 'turn-away', however, is probably a preferable manoeuvre in aircraft without front movable guns. With these aircraft it may not be possible to turn inwards sufficiently to bring

---

MEMORIES OF MALTA

The late Air Marshal Sir Ivor Broom KCB CBE DSO DFC** AFC recalled his time as a sergeant pilot flying Blenheims from Malta, in an interview with François Prins:

We carried out all manner of missions; they were sometimes quite long flights. Malta was a sort of aircraft carrier in the Med and from there we could range to the coast of Libya, southern Italy and Sicily. In between were the enemy ships; convoys taking supplies to Rommel. That was what we were after, especially the fuel tankers. If Rommel had no fuel he could not use his vehicles and tanks.

I arrived in Malta in early September 1941, so I was there later than those who had been battling for months before. I was supposed to be on my way to Egypt, but was effectively 'shanghaied'! My first mission was against the barracks at Homs. Sadly, two aircraft collided, one was the CO, Wing Commander Scivier, and his aircraft crashed, but the other flown by Sgt Williams made it back having bombed the target.

What Ivor Broom did not mention was that on the way back to Malta the damaged aircraft was lagging behind and was in a bad way; it had bent propellers and a missing pitot tube following the collision. Consequently, Williams had no way of knowing his airspeed or altitude. Broom went back and escorted the badly vibrating Blenheim home to Luqa, and his observer signalled speed and altitude with an Aldis lamp to the other aircraft. When they approached the runway at Luqa, Broom flew alongside Williams's aircraft to guide him on to the runway before he turned and landed himself.

front fixed guns to bear, whereas with a 'turn-away' the movable guns may be able to be effectively brought into action.

Attack from the sun

In all attacks it is necessary to keep the enemy in sight from the earliest possible moment, so that the correct time to turn-in to throw off the fighter can be accurately judged. If the bombers are surprised, then it will be too late to produce any effective evasion. For this reason it cannot be too strongly stressed that when the sun is visible, anti-glare spectacles should be worn by all air gunners and by as many more of the crew as supplies will permit.

Summary

The following defensive formations and manoeuvres have been found to be effective:
(a) *Section.*
    (i) Undulating of the formation in unison, or by aircraft individually.
    (ii) Turning-in formation.
    (iii) Corkscrewing.
(b) *Flight of six.*
    (i) Two sections in close support, manoeuvring as in (a) (i) or (ii).
    (ii) Sliding sections, the rear section passing to and fro close astern of, and below or above, the leading section.
(c) *Squadron of nine.*
    (i) Three sections in close vic, manoeuvring as in (a) (i) or (ii) or (b) (ii).

Low flying

It will often be desirable to carry out low attacks preceded and followed up by low flying in the approach and in the 'get away'. Light AA, small arms and machine-gun fire have all been found to be effective up to a height of 3,000ft and above. If aircraft fly really low, under 200ft, the AA gunner's fields of view and fire are so restricted and the rate of change of angle may be so high that the aircraft becomes a most difficult target. Sinking will add appreciably to the security of the target.

A low-flying bomber is not easily detected by fighters, and their freedom of manoeuvre is reduced. They are, moreover, unable to exploit the Blenheim's blind areas. If the bomber is very close to the ground, the fighter is restricted to a

different approach from astern and above. This provides an unobstructed target for the rear gun, and reduces the area which the bomber must keep under observation.

The low-flying bomber is least vulnerable when hedge-hopping with sudden jinks, but this necessitates appreciable individual liberty of action which makes formation flying impracticable. Its utility may therefore be greatest in the 'get away' after a dive-bombing or low-level attack. If used as an approach for low-level bombing with heavy bombs, aircraft will probably have to 'drop' independently at minimum intervals of some 30 seconds so as to ensure that they are not damaged by the delay action bombs of preceding aircraft. In the presence of powerful defences against low flying it would be undesirable to form close sections prior to the delivery of the attack.

Fighting control

All personnel of the formation should search for enemy aircraft and sighting reports should be made to the formation leader.

It is essential in defence that the timing of manoeuvre and fire should be controlled by the air gunner of the leader's aircraft who is best placed to observe both his own formation and enemy aircraft when attack is imminent.

The change from cruising to defensive formation will be ordered by the formation leader on information given by the leading air gunner.

ABOVE The gun-firing button on the control wheel of a Blenheim Mk IVF was operated by the pilot's right thumb. *(Air Ministry)*

The manoeuvres to be adopted in any given circumstances will be decided by the formation leader who will inform the leading air gunner.

Responsibilities of the leading air gunner

The responsibilities of the leading air gunner will be:

(a) To give adequate and timely information of the enemy's manoeuvres to the formation leader. To be most effective, manoeuvre should begin before fire is opened by the fighters. A suitable time for the Messerschmitt 109 is probably when fighters are at about 300 yards range.

(b) To indicate targets, where necessary, to be engaged by one or more air gunners, and to check any tendency to open fire prematurely, since accuracy of fire is necessary to achieve effect.

Fighting control of sections may be delegated to section leader's air gunners at the discretion of the formation leader.

As the leading air gunner may become a casualty, it is advisable to appoint a deputy, possibly the deputy formation leader's air gunner, accepting the disadvantage that control is not then exercised from the formation leader's aircraft.

Avoidance of high-altitude anti-aircraft fire

The lethal range of fragmentation of single bursts may be some 40 yards, but the zone of error makes a distance of about 200 yards between sections advisable at a height of 10,000ft.

Anti-aircraft fire does not utilise observation of previous rounds. Each shot is treated as a separate problem, solved with the aid of the predictor, and the first burst, therefore, may be effective if avoiding action has not been taken.

A sequence of changes for the passage of an AA-defended area should be detailed before flight. For example, a formation at a height of 15,000ft and a speed of 200mph could change course 4° every 35 seconds in the following order – Right, Climb, Left, Dive. After AA fire is opened, the changes would be 6° every 20 seconds.

It should be remembered that, when German fighters are in the vicinity, AA gunners often draw their attention to a bomber formation by firing a series of bursts pointing towards the formation.

Over clouds

When aircraft are flying over clouds, AA fire can only be directed by sound. Owing to the time the sound takes to reach the detectors and the time taken to obtain an estimate of the aircraft's speed, avoiding action need be much less frequent. If aircraft change course 5° every 1½ minutes, never maintaining a constant height, they should avoid the first burst. When bursts are observed, changes of course of 5° may be made every 45 seconds.

Another method used by AA gunners when an aircraft cannot be seen is to put up a barrage around it. Many barrages will be wide and will necessitate no additional manoeuvres. Some, however, may be uncomfortably close.

If the position of the centre of the group of bursts can be approximately estimated, the aircraft should manoeuvre away in the opposite direction.

If this position is not apparent, the following considerations should be borne in mind. An AA shell burst is more dangerous below than above. Although the blast effect from a near miss in any position will be the same, the fragments from an 'over' never hit an aircraft, but those from a 'short' may do so. A loss of height is therefore normally more effective than a gain of height. Again, bursts are more dangerous in front than behind, as the danger zone is bigger when flying into the fragments than when flying away from them. Hence an increase in speed will normally be more effective than a decrease in speed.

Defensive tactics – night

Although the Blenheim bomber has not been used extensively in night operations, the possibility of it being so used is ever present, and should not, therefore, be overlooked. The tactics of night operations are fully dealt with in CD119, and this information is intended to supersede the manual. It does, however, incorporate up-to-date knowledge of German tactics, and is written with particular reference

to the Blenheim, operating independently at night.

There are three types of opposition to be expected by night-flying aircraft; searchlights, AA guns and fighters.

Searchlights

Searchlights are used to illuminate bombers so that:

(a) AA gunners can use their normal prediction methods.
(b) The bomber's position may be indicated to fighters.
(c) The bomber's crew may be so dazzled that they cannot see fighters, and in addition may lose control of the aircraft through not being able to see the instruments.

Searchlights have also recently been used to obscure targets from the view of bombers by concentrating them in the form of a cone with the apex over the centre of the target, thus dazzling the crew of the bomber. The dazzle effect is often accentuated by drifting smoke and haze.

A searchlight is trained initially with the aid of sound locators, but once it has picked up an aircraft, is trained by sight. As sound travels about 1,000ft per second, the sound locator never points at the present position of an aircraft, but at a past position, where the aircraft was when it emitted the sound. For example, sound takes about 10 seconds to travel 11,000ft. In this time an aircraft flying at 150mph travels 2,200ft. As the diameter of a normal searchlight beam at 11,000ft is about 550ft, a large allowance is necessary. Searchlight crews make this allowance by guessing the aircraft's speed, or by having lines of sound locators at a definite interval to measure its speed.

It will be apparent that it is much more difficult for the searchlight to make its first contact than to hold an aircraft subsequently. A bomber's tactics should, therefore, be designed primarily to avoid being picked up by the searchlight, rather than to escape from the beam after having been picked up. This is particularly important in view of the fact that German AA guns may be fired, and searchlights exposed, *at the same time*, working on invisible prediction by the sound locators. Bomber crews should, therefore, be fully prepared for a burst of AA fire immediately the searchlights come on, and take as violent avoiding action as possible.

Avoiding action

To avoid being picked up, the time lag inherent in any sound-locating system can be exploited. Whatever system is in use, it will probably be necessary for locators to follow an aircraft for some time before the searchlight can be switched on with any probability of illuminating the target. If, therefore, an aircraft continually changes course, the searchlight should fail to find it. A change of height does not affect the problem, as the aircraft would not thereby escape the beam. The best avoiding action appears to be to change course about 5° every 1½ minutes when over a suspected searchlight zone.

Desynchronisation of engines will probably confuse an inexperienced sound locator operator temporarily, but will not be effective against a trained operator. This stratagem is not, therefore, a substitute for the avoiding action described above.

An aircraft with its engine throttled back is normally inaudible above 6,000ft, and at greater heights should remain inaudible with partial throttle. Advantage of this can be taken by approaching and passing over a defended area in a shallow glide. In this way large distances can be covered without much loss of height.

Visibility

Recent experience has confirmed that, in normal circumstances, an aircraft painted with anti-reflection paint on the undersurfaces, is invisible from the ground in a searchlight beam, at heights above 12,000ft. Instances have occurred of German searchlights being dowsed, although illuminating an aircraft when flying above this height. When illuminated by searchlights at 12,000ft or above, therefore, normal avoiding action should be sufficient to take an aircraft clear of the lights.

It must not be assumed, however, that the aircraft will also be invisible to a nearby fighter, and a close lookout will be necessary.

At lower heights, when an aircraft is held in a searchlight beam and can be seen from the ground, attacks by AA guns and/or fighters can be expected shortly after. As these attacks will be dependent for their effectiveness on searchlight illumination of the target, it is of first importance to escape from the beam. Alterations in height are not in themselves effective except in so much as they involve alterations of speed. The best avoiding action is to make a steep turn and increase speed. It may sometimes be advisable to lose a little height to gain speed. Alternatively, if the aircraft

is near the limit of visibility, it might be advisable to make climbing turns so as to reach invisibility height. If below 3,000ft and the beams cannot be shaken off, it may be advantageous to lose height since searchlights cannot easily be traversed quickly enough to follow an aircraft very low down.

The German defence system includes an outer screen of Flak ships in the North Sea. These ships cannot be as efficient as sound locators on land. The sound of waves and wind combined with the instability of a ship make accurate sound locating almost impossible except in a flat calm. In fact it is questionable whether high-flying aircraft could be heard at all, especially if throttled back slightly. The ships will, therefore, not normally be able to give warning of the approach of high-flying aircraft.

Anti-aircraft guns

If a bomber can be seen in searchlight beams, AA gunners follow normal daylight prediction methods. The method of escaping a beam given above is more violent than the avoiding action necessary against AA fire in daylight and will, therefore, be effective against night AA fire.

In other cases, when a bomber is either too high to be seen in searchlight beams, or is above cloud, avoiding action similar to that taken above clouds in the daytime is necessary.

Fighters

A fighter's greatest difficulty at night is to find the bomber at all. The position of bombers is often indicated to fighters by the intersection of searchlight beams and by AA fire. Searchlight beams ahead of a bomber may be used to silhouette it to a fighter approaching from behind.

When an aircraft is not held in a searchlight beam, it can be seen much more easily from below than from above. A fighter's best approach is, therefore, from slightly below and behind. He is unable to close quickly as in daylight owing to the difficulty in judging range and closing speed, but will try to stalk the bomber, drawing gradually closer to get to point-blank range. A very close lookout must be maintained by the bomber crew in the restricted area of fighter approach below and astern. Night glasses may help to ensure that the fighter is seen in time.

The main counter to fighter attack at night must be evasion. When a fighter is seen or opens fire, the bomber must immediately dive and turn steeply away. A loss of as little as 500ft should shake off the fighter who will probably never regain contact. It must be emphasised that it is useless to restrict manoeuvre in order to give the rear gunner a good shot. At height a fighter can approach so closely before being seen that he has a big advantage over the bomber in a shooting match. On the other hand, it is so difficult to keep the bomber in view, that evasive action by the bomber should always be successful, *if taken in time*.

Intercommunication between the rear gunner and the pilot must be rapid and certain. It should be noted that, under no circumstances, should a bomber, when diving and turning, open up the engines. On the contrary, they should be kept well throttled back. Opening the throttles beyond zero boost results in a great increase in the exhaust flame. At full throttle this flame can easily be seen from a distance of one mile.

Summary

The following action is recommended:

(i) An attempt should be made to get far into a defended area undetected, by losing height, partially throttled back.

(ii) When flying over a defended zone, a change of course of 5° every 1½ minutes should be made, and height should be continually varied.

(iii) If caught in a beam over 12,000ft or above cloud, the same changes of course should be continued.

(iv) If caught in a beam within visibility height, turns should be made, and speed increased, or climbing turns to invisibility height should be made.

(v) If in an AA barrage, a turn in the opposite direction from the centre of the group should be made. If in doubt, speed should be increased and height lost.

(vi) When a fighter is seen in position to attack, a diving turn should be made for about 500ft.

The bomber's task is to get to the target

The avoiding action recommended above is purely defensive and is designed to increase the chance of reaching the target. It must not be carried out to such an extent that the main offensive task is prejudiced. LOSSES OF HEIGHT AND DEVIATIONS FROM TRACK CAUSED BY EVASIVE MANOEUVRES MUST THEREFORE BE MADE GOOD AT THE FIRST OPPORTUNITY.

No 13 SQUADRON BISLEY SORTIE

This collection of pictures was taken by Sergeant Hector Cunliffe Thornton of the Photographic Section at RAF Souk-el-Arba, Tunisia, in 1943. They show the daily routine to fly a Blenheim Mk V 'Bisley' anti-submarine/shipping escort sortie by 13 Squadron, which took place on 1 August 1943.

1 The commanding officer receives the daily programme.

2 He then compiles the squadron daily programme and discusses it with one of his flight commanders.

3 The daily programme is ready to be sent to the orderly room.

4 Clerks in the orderly room then type a stencil copy, check the details and phone them through to the relevant sections on the base.

5 The squadron navigation officer briefs the crew.

6 The navigator (left) studies the area to be patrolled and discusses it with his pilot.

7 The senior controller gives the crew their final details and the maps are checked.

8 The senior controller then points out the final area to be patrolled.

9 In the control room the movements board shows this sortie, with Flight Lieutenant Thorburn as captain, scheduled to take off at 14:15hrs in aircraft 'X' of 13 Squadron. The Bisley is due on patrol at 15:00hrs, off patrol at 17:45hrs and set to return to base at 18:15hrs, totalling four hours airborne.

10 The navigator plots the course for the sortie.

11 The signal officer briefs the wireless operator.

12 The navigator collects a camera.

13 The aircrew collect their flying kit, including 'Mae Wests' and parachutes.

14 They then climb aboard a truck which will take them out to dispersal.

15 The pilot signs for his aircraft in the flight office.

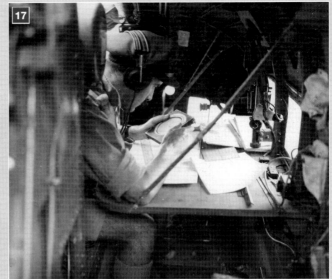

16 The crew load their kit aboard 13 Squadron Blenheim Mk V 'X'.

17 The navigator checks his compass and lays his maps out at his station in the nose of the Blenheim Mk V.

18 The wireless operator/air gunner checks his turret and guns.

19 The pilot checks for full and free movement of his controls.

20 Port engine running OK, contact starboard.

21 Chocks away, brakes off and the pilot prepares to taxi out to the runway.

22 Taxying along a dusty peri-track on the airfield.

23 The Blenheim gets airborne ready to set course for its patrol area over the sea.

24 Four hours later the Blenheim has returned to base safely, and the groundcrew calls for the pilot to stop.

25 A post-sortie interrogation is carried out by the intelligence officer, and the navigator points out where the crew's Blenheim escorted shipping.

'I counted myself lucky to be involved in what I believed to be an iconic aircraft, but little did I realise then that I would still be involved some 35 years and three Blenheim projects later!'

John 'Smudge' Smith, member of the restoration team, Blenheim Mk I L6739.

Chapter Six

The engineer's view

From 2015, aviation enthusiasts will be able to see a Blenheim flying at public air shows for the first time in 12 years, and a Blenheim Mk I in the air for the first time since the Second World War. However, this does not happen by the pilot just turning up and flying the aircraft. A large team of skilled aero engineers, volunteers and support staff need to have restored the aircraft for countless hours, ensured it is in good condition to fly on the day, refuelled it, towed it out of the hangar and assisted the pilot with the start-up.

OPPOSITE Fitters work on a B Flight Blenheim Mk V out in the searing heat at Souk-el-Arba, Tunisia, in 1943. *(Sergeant Hector Cunliffe Thornton/No 13 Squadron Archives)*

This chapter looks at some of the work needed to keep a Blenheim in the air. The information that follows does not cover all the work that is involved in the handling and general preparation of a Blenheim; however, it is intended that the main essential operations are described.

Safety first!

Any aircraft should be treated with respect, even when on static display as there are still solid, sharp edges which could cause injury. However, a wartime bomber with two propellers requires a special mindset with regards to safety, and even when static an airworthy example should be treated as 'live'. Prior to moving a propeller a fellow crew member in the cockpit should confirm to the groundcrew personnel on the exterior that the magneto switches are in the 'off' position, otherwise there could be a potential risk that the engine could fire-up.

Prior to starting the engines great care must be taken to ensure that no unauthorised personnel are close to the aircraft, as a turning propeller blade can easily be fatal to the unwary. A fast-turning three-bladed metal propeller is a lethal instrument even to those familiar with its dangers. The differences between groundcrew operations with a propeller-driven aircraft and one with jet engines are significant, so even someone with vast experience with jets should not be complacent. However, one common practice remains the same and is worthy of note – as long as the chocks are in place on the aircraft's main wheels, it will not be moving forward!

Fortunately one consideration that the groundcrews of currently airworthy Second World War aircraft do not need to worry about any longer is that of a live armed aeroplane.

Standard safety equipment, such as sturdy boots with a good grip on the sole, ear defenders, protective gloves and overalls are essential to protect the groundcrew from spillage, noise, slipping and other injuries.

While replenishing oils and greases, care must be taken to ensure that the product being used is of the correct consistency, otherwise mechanical damage could result. The engineer must make careful checks of this, as the containers can be very similar in appearance.

As with aircrew, any engineers entering a prepped-for-flight aircraft must ensure that all their pockets are emptied to prevent the risk of 'Foreign Object Damage' (FOD), as there are so many flying controls that could be inhibited by an unseen obstruction.

Tools and working facilities

A good set of BA and BSF spanners and sockets is essential, as is a good general-purpose tool kit including screwdrivers, locking pliers and wire cutters. Specialist tools, such as box and peg spanners for stripping components and rigging boards for setting up flying controls, are also required.

An aircraft such as this twin-engined bomber also demands a spacious hangar. The aircraft may need to be split, the turret may have to be lifted out, or an engine may require removal and refitting, and the ARC hangar allows all such actions to be carried out.

A hydraulic rig is necessary to perform flap

BELOW The dedicated spares rack and toolbox for Bolingbroke G-BPIV in the ARC hangar at Duxford. *(Jarrod Cotter)*

and undercarriage system functions, and wheel chariots are needed to allow the removal of the Blenheim's mainwheel units. Lastly, engine staging allows work to be carried out while the engines are in place at a relatively high level on the wings.

Towing

Towing eyes are provided on the inboard leg of each undercarriage unit and at tailwheel fork ends. In no instance should the Blenheim be towed from the rear by a tractor. The arm for steering the tailwheel is attached to the tailwheel axle fittings. Picketing eyes are provided at the outboard end of the centre mainplane front spar.

Refuelling

Access to the filler caps for replenishing the fuel and oil tanks is as follows:

(i) Fuel – the hinged filler caps on the fuel tanks are accessible by removing the cover plates in the centre and outer mainplanes. In wartime the centre plane fuel tanks were replenished with DTD 230 fuel, and the outer tanks with 100-octane fuel.

(ii) Oil – the oil tank filler caps are accessible through doors on the engine nacelle

LEFT The ARC hangar facilities allow for all essential maintenance tasks to be carried out in order to keep the Blenheim airworthy. Here, following an early ground run, G-BPIV's port engine has been removed from the aircraft during mid-August 2014, and a leaking cylinder head and piston are on the bench for attention. In the background chief engineer 'Smudge' Smith works on the area of the engine from which the cylinder head has been removed. *(Jarrod Cotter)*

BELOW A Finnish Blenheim Mk I being towed by a caterpillar-tracked tractor on a snowy Luonetjärvi airfield in late March 1944. Note the member of the groundcrew at the rear, who is steering the aircraft with the dedicated arm for turning the tailwheel, which is attached to the axle fittings. *(SA-Kuva)*

JOHN 'SMUDGE' SMITH

John Smith, familiarly known as 'Smudge', has been involved with all three Blenheim restorations to flight. Here he describes his more than 35 years of working on this iconic aircraft.

In 1979, while I was visiting IWM Duxford, I heard that the Blenheim team were looking for a volunteer detail metal worker. Having been in the RAF and in Research and Development for the then Ministry of Aviation, and looking for a hobby involving aircraft, I was fortunate to be introduced to those involved.

I was just six years old at the end of the Second World War, so these aircraft were as they say 'in the blood', and as a youngster I had built various model aircraft, the Blenheim being one of them. I counted myself lucky to be involved in what I believed to be an iconic aircraft, but little did I realise then that I would still be involved some 35 years and three Blenheim projects later!

As a young man I was fortunate enough to be taught by some very highly skilled and competent craftsmen in the manufacture of airframe assemblies and I trained and worked on types of airframes similar to the Blenheim, so I was more than pleased to be able to put these skills to good use in manufacturing parts for the Blenheim and later other vintage aircraft. The Blenheim was most certainly the largest project undertaken

at that time and a good many people were of the opinion that it couldn't be done, but we are a determined group and I was fortunate to work with a highly skilled and dedicated team of volunteers. By this time John Romain had taken on the job of full-time engineer in charge of the project and it moved forward under his guidance and that of the then owner, Graham Warner.

It's a tremendous learning curve to completely restore an aircraft of this nature and working with the minimum amount of information, as all we had was the Canadian Bolingbroke manual and the AP1530B parts manual that gives the material specifications, but no manufacturing drawings. In spite of the misgivings of certain sections of the industry, some 12 years later we launched the Blenheim Mk IV (Bolingbroke IV-T 10038) on 20 May 1987. Unfortunately, as is well documented, the Blenheim was destroyed at Denham one month later on 21 June 1987. I, along with John Romain, was one of the crew on board and we counted ourselves lucky to survive the accident. The reason for this crash is well known and no further discussion is needed here, apart from to say there was no mechanical fault.

The team members were devastated by the loss of the aircraft after so many thousands of hours of work, but we were determined that we would have our Blenheim so we obtained another Bolingbroke (10201) and set to giving ourselves five years to complete the task. Having had the experience of the first restoration we were able to make good progress on this project. Only a little of the first aircraft was useable so the majority of the work had to be done all over again, but we completed the task in the five years that we allotted ourselves with the aircraft flying in May 1993. By this time the Aircraft Restoration Company had been set up and a number of the volunteers were now working for the company full time, including myself.

One of the satisfying results of this type of restoration is that we took some younger members on to the volunteer team and they were able to learn the skills of yesteryear, and have now become quite senior members of the company.

BELOW John 'Smudge' Smith in the cockpit of L6739. 'Smudge' has been a stalwart member of the Blenheim team and has been involved with all three of the restorations to flight over a period of more than 35 years. *(Jarrod Cotter)*

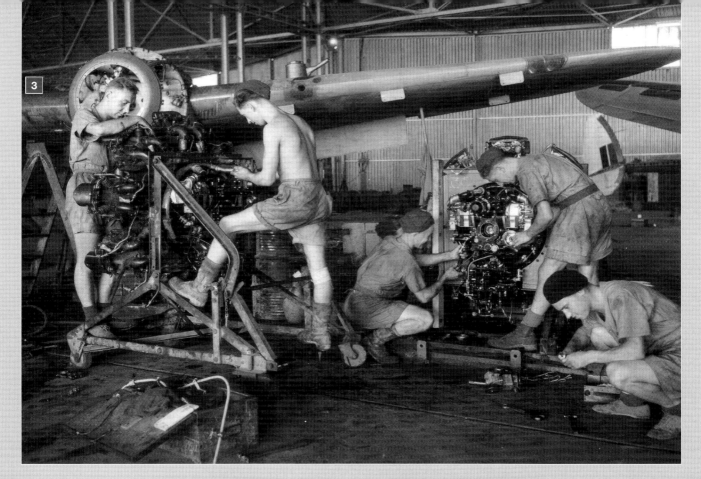

a pressure of 400lb/in^2. The legs should be fully extended during this operation. This charging pressure corresponds to a statically compressed oleo-leg pressure of 525lb/in^2 for an all-up weight of 14,400lb. After charging, all the valves should be securely tightened on their seats and the dust cap replaced on the air valve. The locking plate on the gland nut must be in position.

Replacement of packing rings – if excessive oil leakage occurs the packing rings must be renewed. For this operation the wheel and axle must be removed from the oleo frame and the oleo frame detached from the aeroplane. To renew the packing rings the procedure is as follows:

(i) Unscrew the oil level plug slowly.
(ii) When the air has ceased to escape, remove the plug, the safety lock and the locking eye.
(iii) Unscrew the wheel axle bearing from the lower end of the sustaining ram after removing the locking bolt.
(iv) Unscrew and withdraw the gland nut together with the gland bearing sleeve.
(v) Withdraw the sustaining ram. If this is difficult, the sustaining ram may be forced out by pumping oil through the air valve after replacing the oil level plug.
(vi) Before beginning reassembly, wash all parts in paraffin and allow to drain.
(vii) Shut the air valve and the oil plug, invert the cylinder and pour in the quantity of oil specified on the instruction plate.
(viii) Insert the sustaining ram, taking care not to spill any oil.
(ix) Tap the new packing rings into position with a hardwood drift, taking care not to damage the feather edge of the ring. The rings should previously have been soaked in oil, anti-freezing, type A, for at least 12 hours.
(x) Tighten the gland nut to bed the rings into place and then loosen half a turn.
(xi) Refit the locking eye, safety lock and other details.

Adjustment of hydraulic jack travel – in order to check the travel of the hydraulic jack in relation to the retracted and extended positions of the undercarriage structure, the procedure detailed below should be followed:

(i) Jack up the aeroplane on trestles.
(ii) Retract the undercarriage.
(iii) Check the clearance of the top latch. These clearances should be as follows:
(a) The moving latch should have a minimum clearance from the fixed latch of 0.015in when the jack is at the end of its stroke.
(b) The moving latch must clear the structure in all positions.
(iv) Adjust the jacks, if necessary, to give clearances by fitting washers (Part No BS1800) between the gland nut and the stop.
(v) Lower the undercarriage.
(vi) Disconnect the jack by removing the bolt connecting the jack to the undercarriage structure.
(vii) Apply the full hydraulic pressure to the jacks.
(viii) Check the pin hold in the crosshead at the lower end of the piston rod for alignment with the hole in the star fitting of the undercarriage structure.
(ix) Adjust the length of the piston rod by the crosshead to bring the excess travel of the jack within the limits of +0.015in to +0.030in. To effect this adjustment it may be necessary to reduce the thickness of the locknut, but in no case may the thickness after adjustment be less than $\frac{5}{16}$in.
(x) Refit the bolt connecting the jack to the undercarriage structure.
(xi) Restore the aeroplane to normal.

In most instances it will be possible to effect adjustment as described above, but when the required adjustment is beyond the limit stated it will be necessary to substitute for the existing jack a new one (Part No BS1300) having a shorter piston rod (Part No BS4177).

Test for undercarriage hydraulic lock plunger – after a period of service the undercarriage hydraulic locks tend to creep, due to frictional losses. It is essential, therefore, to test these locks periodically. The testing of the locking plungers may be carried out while they are in place – and without draining the hydraulic system – by means of a test rig. The resistance to movement offered by the piston when under test should not be below 60–70lb, the total of the incremental loads applied being recorded on the spring balance.

If the hydraulic locking plunger extends prematurely, the gland nut at each end of the lock should be tightened until the correct load can be obtained. If tightening the nuts does not give the required frictional resistance to plunger movement, a new gland packing must be fitted. When replacing the catch actuating rod, care should be exercised to ensure that the bolt and nut connecting the aft end of the actuating rod to the catch are replaced in such a manner as to prevent fouling of the corresponding top and bottom catch connecting tube. Care should also be taken not to overtighten the bolt and to ensure that there is sufficient freedom of movement between the actuating rod and the locking catch.

Wheel tyres – the main undercarriage and the tailwheel tyres should be kept inflated to a pressure of $50lb/in^2$ and $45lb/in^2$ respectively. These pressures should be checked with a gauge.

Hydraulic fluid

The fluid used in the system is oil, anti-freezing, type A (Stores Ref. 34A/43 and 46).

Draining – the bulk of the oil can be removed by uncoupling a union low down in the system; the undercarriage jacks should be in the 'up' position. By taking out the venting screws, the fluid in the jack may be removed.

Filling – if a portable pump is available it should be connected to the standpipe connection on the rear face of the fireproof bulkhead near the fluid reservoir and employed to pump the fluid into the system. While the pump is working, the jacks should be operated in turn several times to the full extent of their travel; to do this without jacking up the aeroplane, withdraw the bolt securing the undercarriage jack at the undercarriage frame star fitting. When the system is filled with fluid all the jacks should be moved to the extended position and the reservoir topped up to the level of the filler. It is important that this level should be maintained otherwise air may be drawn into the system. If the hand pump is used for filling, the fluid should be poured into the reservoir, keeping the level constantly up to the filler. The above procedure should ensure that all the air is expelled from the system, but if its pressure is indicated by backlash in the moving parts, venting must be carried out.

Venting – if venting is necessary, the venting screws should be slackened and the fluid circulated by the hand pump. The venting screws should be tightened again when no further air bubbles issue at the screws.

Leakage – slight leakage from the glands and the pipe unions may be checked by gently tightening the gland or union nuts, but excessive tightening must be avoided for fear of damage to the packings and pipe flares.

Pipeline joints – each pipe coupling consists of a tube nut, a flared pipe and an adaptor which provides a core seating. For the method of re-flaring pipe ends, reference should be made to the section of AP1464A dealing with metal couplings.

Cleaning – the filter should be cleaned shortly after the system is filled with fresh fluid. The undercarriage mechanism should be kept free from the accumulation of mud, especially at the laps for the engine nacelle cover in the retracted position and at the knee joints of the radius struts. The undercarriage locking catches must be examined periodically to ensure that they drop freely into place. In damp weather they should be cleared of mud and grit and lubricated after each flight.

Pneumatic system

This system supplies power to the wheel brakes, the control for the Browning machine gun, the camera gun control and the fuel jettison control. The system comprises an engine-driven air compressor, an oil reservoir, an oil trap, an air container, a charging connection T-piece, an air filter, a camera gun control connection, a fuel jettison control valve, fuel jettison actuating cocks and an automatic air supply cut-out valve for the fuel jettison control cocks. The charging connection is situated in the fuselage, on the starboard side, between and above the front and rear spars. The maximum charging pressure of the air container is $200lb/in^2$.

When the pressure in the system is reduced to $70lb/in^2$, the cut-out valve automatically closes and thus retains in the system sufficient pressure to ensure correct functioning of the brakes.

Wheel brake units – each port and starboard brake unit is of the Dunlop type and consists of a rimmed disc which is bolted to the brake unit torque flange integral with the inboard sleeve on the axle. Full details of the construction and

ABOVE **Members of the groundcrew of a 404 Squadron RCAF Blenheim of Coastal Command at Dyce in Scotland, get the aircraft in good shape before a sortie. Corporal H.B. McFarlane (left) checks the port engine which has just been prepared by Aircraftman R. Krantz, while Corporal M. Smith checks the port mainwheel.** *(404 Squadron RCAF)*

operation of the Dunlop-type brake units are given in the relevant part of AP1464B, Volume 1.

Wheel brake system – the wheel brake system comprises two pneumatic brake units, a Dunlop-type dual relay valve with link and lever control mechanism and operating cable, a triple air pressure gauge and necessary tubing and coupling. Full details of the construction and operation of the dual relay valve control unit, and a general description of the pneumatic brake system are given in the relevant part of AP1464B, Volume 1.

Mechanical remote controls

When a new length of conduit is fitted, or existing conduit is replaced after removal from the end fittings or box units, care must be taken to replace the locking pin which, together with a clamp bolt, secures the conduit in position. If a new length of conduit is fitted, the conduit must be pushed into position in the clamp and a drill passed through the existing holes in the clamp to clear a passage for the pin.

Cowling fasteners

When replacing cowling panels fitted with the Bristol-type cowling fastener, ensure that the bottom flat plate, supported on washers adjacent to the cowling panel, has not been bowed, and that the four centre pops on the U-plate of the bracket are prominent and effective. If the flat plate has been bowed, this may be rectified by inserting a screwdriver or similar tool under the plate and levering it up.

The centre pops may be enlarged by a centre punch if necessary. The plain washer under the castle nut of the cowling fastener is to be removed and replaced by a double-spring washer to make the catch more effective, and the split pin is to be retained in the existing hole.

Throttle control lever adjustment

Care must be taken in adjusting the throttle levers. The clamping screw on the inboard face of the control quadrant must be screwed up until the force required to move each throttle lever independently is approximately 8½lb. This force must be tested by means of a spring balance, the pull being applied just below the knob on the lever. The balance should read not less than 8lb when the lever commences to move. Subsequently, if a pilot suspects by 'feel' of the control that it has slackened, he must take the necessary action to have it readjusted.

Carburettor cut-out control adjustment

If the carburettor cut-out control does not return to the fully open position after being operated to stop the engine, there will be hesitancy when the throttle is opened, or complete failure of the engine to respond to the throttle, often accompanied by back-firing. This will be due to the compression spring, located between the bulkhead and a collar on the airframe part of the control, being fully extended before it has returned the cut-out control to the fully open position. This spring must therefore be so adjusted that it is under considerable compression even when the cut-out valves are fully open, thus ensuring that the spring will hold the valves in the fully open position except when the control is operated to stop the engine.

Air-intake shutter control

If the cable from the air-intake shutter to the bell-crank lever on the engine mounting becomes too slack, the shutter will not operate efficiently. The method of correction is as follows:
(i) Set the levers in the pilot's cabin to the 'Hot air' position.
(ii) Examine the air-intake shutters. These should be fully closed. If they remain partially open, the control system is not functioning correctly.

(iii) Examine the security of the two clips which carry the MR controls and the bell-crank lever. These clips are bolted to the engine mounting lower tube (inboard port, outboard starboard). If either of these clips has moved due to the loosening of the attachment bolts, they should be repositioned by moving the clip along the engine mounting tube until the air-intake shutter closes. If neither clip appears to have moved out of position, the forward clip should be loosened and moved up the tube until the air-intake shutter closes.

(iv) Check the setting by operating the levers in the pilot's cabin.

(v) Secure the clip attachment bolts firmly.

Cowling gill controls

The cowling gills can be opened through a range of 15°. The method of checking or resetting the gill movement to obtain synchronisation of the port and starboard units is as follows:

(i) Mount the aeroplane in the rigging position.

(ii) Set the handwheel in the pilot's cockpit to the fully closed position.

(iii) Using a clinometer, set the port and the starboard gills to +2°.

(iv) Connect up the chains and the cables.

(v) Open the gills by means of the handwheel until a reading of +17° is obtained on the clinometer. Ensure that the stop in the handwheel unit is home, and that the chains and cables are adjusted to give the full gill movement of 15°.

(vi) Adjust the eccentric sprocket, if necessary, to take up any slackness in the chain drive.

Lubrication

The various points that require lubricating, and the type of lubricant to be used are shown in the relevant illustrations. The following deals briefly with the lubrication of controls:

(i) Control chains – all chains for the various

LUBRICATION DIAGRAM

LEFT A diagram showing the lubrication points on a Blenheim. (Air Ministry)

1 Oleo-leg fulcrum
2 Radius rod knuckle
3 Radius rod hinge pin
4 Oleo-leg fulcrum
5 Radius rod knuckle
6 Radius rod hinge pin
7 Undercarriage wheel hub
8 Rudder bar torque tube top
9 Rudder bar torque tube bottom
10 Flap jack spigot (port side only)
11 Aileron outer bearing
12 Aileron mid bearing
13 Aileron inner bearing
14 Mainplane flap hinge*
15 Centre plane flap hinge*
16 Flap jack piston rod (port side only)
17 Flap control cable dead eye
18 Flap actuating lever
19 Flaps operating tube control link
20 Flap control cable dead eye
21 Rudder bearing bottom
22 Rudder trimming bearing
23 Rudder bearing bottom
24 Elevator hinge outer
25 Elevator hinge inner
26 Elevator trimmer trunnion
27 Torque shaft (outboard)
28 Torque shaft (outboard)
29 Torque shaft (outboard)
30 Torque shaft (inboard)
31 Torque shaft (inboard)
32 Torque shaft (inboard)
33 Undercarriage jack connection rod
34 Tailwheel hub.

(* These points are indicative of the complete hinge run, the entire length being lubricated by oil can.)

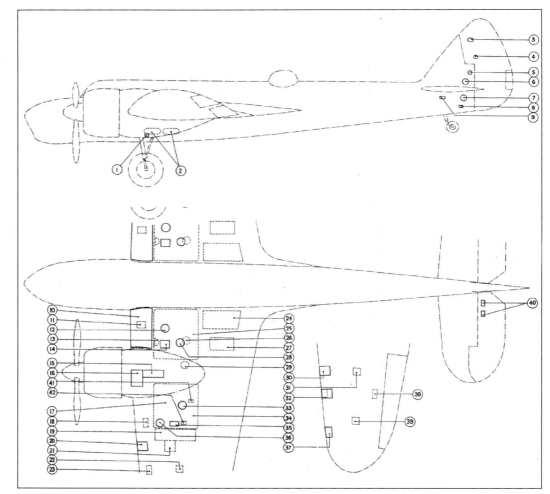

RIGHT A diagram showing the inspection panels on a Blenheim. *(Air Ministry)*

1 Picketing down door on engine nacelle (outboard, port and starboard)
2 Bomb carrier doors (port and starboard)
3 Balance weight rudder (port)
4 Rudder hinge bolt (port)
5 Trimming gear lubrication (port)
6 Trimming gear (port and starboard)
7, 8 and 9 Tailplane fixing bolts (port and starboard)
10 Detachable nosing (general installation inspection)
11 Aileron control (port and starboard)
12 Fuel vent (port and starboard)
13 Fuel cock controls (port and starboard)
14 Fuel filler cap (port and starboard)
15 Oil tank (port and starboard)
16 Oil and hydraulic tanks (port side only)
17 Fuel tank cover door (port and starboard)
18 Aileron control (port and starboard)
19 Gun door (port side only)
20 General inspection (port and starboard)
21 Cartridge box (port side only)
22 General inspection (port and starboard)
23 Aileron controls (port and starboard)
24 Bomb doors (port and starboard)
25 Fuel tank cover door (port and starboard)
26 Fuel sump (port and starboard)
27 Flap controls (port and starboard)
28 Fuel gauge (port and starboard)
29 Fuel pipe connection (port and starboard)
30 General inspection (port and starboard)
31 General inspection (port and starboard)
32 Aileron control (port and starboard)
33 Fuel gauge (port and starboard)
34 Fuel tank cover door (port and starboard)
35 Fuel filler cap (port and starboard)
36 Fuel vent (port and starboard)
37 General inspection (starboard side only)
38 Aileron control (port and starboard)
39 General inspection (port and starboard)
40 Elevator chain and sprocket (port and starboard)
41 Fuel cock controls (port and starboard)
42 Fuel sump (port and starboard).

controls should be kept clean, lubricated and properly tensioned.

(ii) Engine controls – periodically inspect and lubricate all engine controls, the principal points to be lubricated being:
   (a) The bearings of the pilot's control quadrant.
   (b) The bearings and pin-joint couplings of the engine controls between the pilot's control quadrant and the control levers on the engines.
(iii) Propellers – for the lubrication of the variable-pitch propellers, reference should be made to AP1538, Volume 1.

Bomb loading

The two 500lb bombs, the two 250lb LC bombs, or the two 250lb Type B bombs are carried on bomb carriers attached directly to the supports provided in the bomb cells. When four 250lb bombs are carried, a special frame should be installed in the bomb cells. Provision for loading the 250lb smal-bomb container to the 250lb bomb carrier frame on the ground is made to enable the complete unit to be hoisted by means of the bomb-loading winch, thus eliminating the use of the lugs provided on the container. Extreme care should be exercised when loading the container into the carrier by means of the container lifting lugs only. The position of the fuse units should be checked to ensure that they are correctly set for the type of bomb to be loaded.

Bomb-loading winch

In order to load the bombs, a special winch is used. The driving spindle of this is fitted with a ratchet wheel and a hand-controlled pawl. A brake is also fitted to the spindle and automatically applies pressure when unloading a bomb. Before the bomb can descend it will be necessary to turn the operating handle.

LEFT **A drawing of the bomb-loading winch.**
(Air Ministry)

When unloading, the hand-controlled pawl must be lifted from the ratchet. The bomb eye can be centred under the release slip when loading by rocking the winch. This winch may also be used to lift the special frame for the 250lb Type B bombs.

Inspection before loading

Before loading bombs the release system should be checked for correct functioning as follows:

(i) Cock all the electro-magnetic units.

(ii) Close the master control switch.

Close each selector in turn. After testing, set the switch to 'off' before operating a further switch. In each case the jettison lamp should illuminate. If the lamp does not illuminate, one of the following faults may have occurred:

(a) The wiring system between the control panel and the release on the carrier may be faulty.

(b) The connections inside the selector switchbox may have become disconnected.

(c) There may be a broken lamp or a bad connection in the jettison switchbox.

A test lamp connected across the bomb release socket will assist in locating a fault. If the lamp fails to illuminate when the master switch and the selector switch are 'on' and when either the firing switch or the bulb in the jettison switch is pressed, there is a fault in the wiring.

Loading procedure

Two 500lb bombs: The 500lb GP, SAP or AS bombs are carried on two No 2 universal carriers attached directly to the supports in the bomb cell. To load these bombs the procedure is as follows:

(i) Pull the spring-loaded doors down into the open position and secure them with the bomb door stays.

ABOVE Blenheim Mk IV R3600 of 110 Squadron undergoes a full range of servicing for this publicity photograph taken at RAF Wattisham, Suffolk, in June 1940. Armourers unload 250lb GP bombs and small-bomb containers (SBCs) of incendiaries from a trolley, while other groundcrew refuel the aircraft and attend to the engines, the cockpit and the gun turret, accompanied by the squadron mascot sitting on the engine cowling. *(Air Ministry)*

LEFT AND BELOW A series of three pictures showing Finnish Air Force armourers loading a Blenheim Mk I with a payload of 250kg bombs. *(SA-Kuva)*

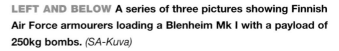

(ii) Open or remove the inspection doors in the sides of the bomb cells.

(iii) Place the bomb on the ground with the support eye under the release slip and place a sling under the bomb, central with the support eye.

(iv) Engage the bomb-loading winch in the cross channel above the release. This operation is carried out inside the fuselage, in the bomb well.

(v) Let the cables down through the holes in the floor and attach the cable hooks to the bomb sling.

(vi) Hoist the bomb into position.

(vii) Adjust the bomb crutches and lock them.

(viii) Verify that the bombs are safe in their slips by pressing the release lever towards the slip. This ensures that the hook of the lever is fully engaged with the recess in the slip toggle bar. The external arm of the release lever assumes an approximately vertical position when the engagement is in position.

(ix) Fit the fuse wires and make the electrical connections.

(x) Close the inspection and the bomb-cell doors.

Two 250lb Type B bombs: When these bombs are carried the bomb-cell doors must be removed. The bombs are carried on two No 1 universal carriers and are loaded as described in the previous procedure.

Four 250lb GP, SAP or AS bombs: These bombs are carried in pairs of No 1 universal carriers that are mounted in a special frame. To load these the procedure is as follows:

(i) Assemble the two bombs, complete with fuses, on the special frame.

(ii) Open or remove the inspection doors.

(iii) Open and secure the bomb-cell doors.

(iv) Place the frame containing the bombs on the ground with the lifting lugs under the hoisting gear.

(v) Attach the hooks on the hoisting cables to the lifting lugs on the cross bar of the frame.

(vi) Hoist the unit into position. (Note: When hoisting or lowering the special frame

with bombs attached, care must be taken to ensure that the crutch adjusters do not foul the inspection doors.)

(vii) See that the locating pegs pass through the locating holes in the fuselage floor.

(viii) Secure from above with the special securing nuts.

(ix) Make the electrical connections.

(x) Close the inspection doors and the bomb-cell doors.

RAE containers: These containers are hoisted in a similar manner to the 500lb bombs describer earlier, except that the bomb sling is not used and the cable hooks are engaged with lugs on each side of the container.

ABOVE An armourer attends to the rearward-firing 0.303in Vickers K-type gas-operated machine gun in a blister-turret fitted under the nose of Blenheim Mk IV R3874 of 110 Squadron at Wattisham, Suffolk, in June 1940. The K gun augmented the Blenheim's main defensive armament in providing some defence against a low rear attack by enemy fighters. (*Air Ministry*)

LEFT Armourers attend to a pair of 0.303in Browning machine guns from the turret of a 404 Squadron Blenheim Mk IV at Dyce, *c*1942. (*No 404 Squadron RCAF*)

Flares: The training flares for forced landing which are carried in the wing roots can be loaded by hand. The spring-loaded doors of the wing root flare compartments must be held open. The reconnaissance flares carried on the light-series carriers on the underside of the fuselage are also loaded by hand.

Practice bombs: These are carried on the light-series carriers which are secured to eyebolts projecting outside the skin, on the underside of the rear fuselage. Stations, which are placed in-line longitudinally, for two light-series carriers are provided. Each light-series carrier can accommodate four practice bombs, making a total of eight in all.

No 13 SQUADRON BISLEY SORTIE – BEHIND THE SCENES

This collection of pictures was taken by Sergeant Hector Cunliffe Thornton of the Photographic Section at RAF Souk-el-Arba, Tunisia, in 1943. They show the daily routines of those who worked behind the scenes to prepare the Blenheim Mk V 'Bisleys' for anti-submarine/shipping escort sorties with 13 Squadron during 1943.

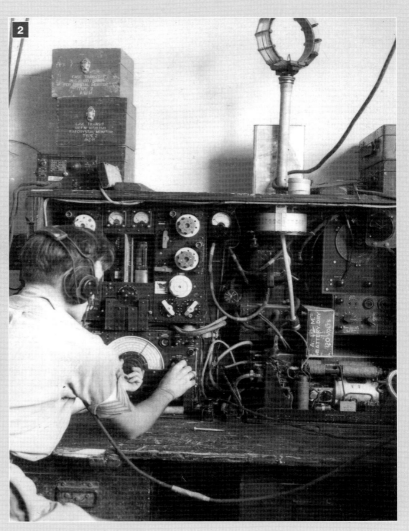

1 An officer aircrew is issued with a new flying helmet from the equipment section.

2 A wireless mechanic carries out tests on a repaired radio set in the wireless section.

3 Vehicles await their next duty at the MT section.

4 A reconnaissance photo taken from a Blenheim Mk V is seen undergoing a final wash after being printed in the Photographic Section.

5 An instrument mechanic at work on a clock, a compass and a turn and slip indicator in the instrument section.

6 Depth charges on a bomb trolley are reversed into place below the bomb bay of a Blenheim Mk V.

7 The depth charges are loaded into the bomb bay by armourers. At this time 13 Squadron was flying anti-submarine patrols.

8 An armourer cleans the gun barrels in the turret of Blenheim Mk V BA997/G.

9 Daily inspections being carried out on a B Flight Blenheim.

10 An A Flight Blenheim Mk V being refuelled.

11 The engineering officer inspects a cylinder head.

12 The aircraft serviceability board being updated with the news that Blenheim Mk V EH353/H is unserviceable and requires an engine change.

13 A fabric worker using a sewing machine in the fabric shop.

Appendix 1

Bristol Blenheim Mk I leading particulars

Duty	Day-bombing.
Type	Twin-engined landplane.
Description	Light bomber with a crew of three (pilot, navigator or bomb-aimer and radio operator or air gunner). Maker's designation, Type 142M.

Principal dimensions	
(Aeroplane in rigging position unless otherwise stated)	
Length overall	39ft 9in
Height to highest point of structure (tail down)	9ft 8in
Height to highest point of structure (rigging position)	14ft 9in
Height to tip of propellers (tail down)	12ft 9½in
Height to tip of propellers (rigging position)	12ft 1in
Span of mainplanes (total)	56ft 4in
Span of centre mainplane (overall)	17ft 11⅞in
Span of outer mainplanes (pin-centre of joints to tip)	19ft 1in
Chord of mainplanes:	
Projected at centre line of aeroplane	11ft 9½in
At root of centre plane	11ft 5¾in
At centre plane outboard ends	8ft 0in
At plane tips	6ft 0in
Projected at tips	4ft 9½in
Aerofoil section	Based on RAF 28 centre line
Incidence of mainplanes to rigging datum	1° ± 0° 15'
Dihedral of mainplanes (measured on datum)	6° 30' ± 0° 15'
Dihedral of mainplanes (measured on top of front spar)	4° 33' ± 0° 15'
Sweepback of centre mainplane	1° 41'
Sweepback of outer mainplanes	6° 11'
Ailerons:	
Span	8ft 2⅝in
Chord (max)	2ft 3in
Flaps:	
Inner span	6ft 9¾in
Outer span	8ft 5in
Elevators:	
Span (including balance)	16ft 3⅞in
Chord (mean – at outboard end of trimming vane)	2ft 3⁷⁄₁₆in
Tailplane:	
Span (total)	16ft 8in
Chord (with elevators, projected on centre line of aeroplane)	5ft 5in
Chord, at root	3ft 5in

Chord (with elevators) projected at tips	4ft 8½in
Chord (elevators removed) at inboard end of tip	2ft 11¾in
Tailplane incidence (normal setting)	-2° to wing incidence or -1° to rigging datum

Areas

Mainplanes, including ailerons	469ft^2 gross
	420ft^2 nett
Ailerons (total – port and starboard)	29.42ft^2
Outer and centre plane flaps (total)	47.0ft^2
Tailplane, without elevators	43.93ft^2
Elevators (total – including trimmer flaps)	32.08ft^2
Elevator trimmer flaps (total)	0.63ft^2
Fin (without rudder)	10.61ft^2
Rudder	25.44ft^2

Weights

Empty	8,100lb
Loaded	12,500lb

Movement of control surfaces

(Linear dimensions measured on chord of arc)

Aileron range of movement at inner end	30° {$^{+2°}$/$_{-0°}$ or 10.22in {$^{+0.6in}$/$_{-0in}$ up
	14° {$^{+0.5in}$/$_{-0.5in}$ or 4.94in {$^{+0.18in}$/$_{-0.18in}$ down
Flap angles:	
For take-off	30° {$^{+2°}$/$_{-0°}$
For landing	60° {$^{+2°}$/$_{-0°}$
Tailplane range of movement	Fixed
Elevator range of movement	33° {$^{+0°}$/$_{-0.83°}$ or 14.183in {$^{+0.0in}$/$_{-0.34in}$ up
	26.5° {$^{+0.5in}$/$_{-0.5in}$ or 11.517in {$^{+0.19in}$/$_{-0.19in}$ down
Elevator trimmer flaps range of movement	25.5° {$^{+1°}$/$_{-1°}$ or 1.48in {$^{+0.06in}$/$_{-0.06in}$ up
	21° {$^{+3°}$/$_{-2°}$ or 1.25in {$^{+0.17in}$/$_{-0.11in}$ down
Rudder range of movement	28.5° {$^{+0.5in}$/$_{-0.5}$ or 18.125in {$^{+0.29in}$/$_{-0.29in}$ port
	28.5° {$^{+0.5in}$/$_{-0.5in}$ or 18.125in {$^{+0.29in}$/$_{-0.29in}$ starboard

Undercarriage

Type	Double oleo-leg single-wheel retractable units
Track	15ft 6in
Shock absorber compression leg	Vickers oleo-pneumatic
Compression leg initial air pressure at full extension	Port legs 365lb/in^2
	Starboard legs 365lb/in^2
Main wheels:	
Wheel type	Dunlop AH419-1
Tyre type	Dunlop 1N 11 Heavy
Tyre pressure	42lb/in^2
Brakes	Dunlop pneumatic

Tailwheel unit

Type	Non-retractable
Shock absorber compression leg	Dowty oleo-pneumatic A3903
Air pressure	410lb/in^2
Wheels:	
Wheel type	Dunlop AH5007
Tyre type	Dunlop 'Ecta' WL11
Tyre pressure	40lb/in^2

Engines (two)	
Type	840hp Bristol Mercury VIII (Mercury XXs are fitted to L6739/ G-BPIV)
Engine thrust incidence to rigging datum	0°
Engine centres (centre line of aeroplane to centre line of engines)	7ft 9in
Fuel	DTD 230/100 octane

Propellers (two)	
Type	de Havilland, variable pitch, 10° pitch range; DIS No 1

Tank capacities	
Fuel	Two tanks in centre mainplane. Each tank 140 gallons. Total 280 gallons
Oil	Two tanks, one in each nacelle. Each tank, 8.5 gallons oil/1 gallon air space. Total 17 gallons of oil

Performance	
Maximum speed	260mph
Cruising speed	200mph
Initial climb rate	1,520ft/min
Range	1,125 miles
Endurance	5.65hrs
Service ceiling	27,280ft

Optimum indicated climbing speeds	
At sea level and up to 8,000ft the optimum indicated climbing speed is 152mph. Above 8,000ft the optimum indicated climbing speed is reduced by 2mph per 1,000ft increase in altitude.	

Correction for position error of airspeed indicator	
At 100mph indicated airspeed	*add* 13.4mph
At 120mph indicated airspeed	*add* 10.5mph
At 140mph indicated airspeed	*add* 8.5mph
At 160mph indicated airspeed	*add* 7.0mph
At 180mph indicated airspeed	*add* 6.0mph
At 200mph indicated airspeed	*add* 5.4mph
At 220mph indicated airspeed	*add* 5.0mph

The all-up weight of the aeroplane during the tests upon which the foregoing climbing speeds and position errors are based was 12,060lb.

Armament	
One fixed Browning 0.303in forward-firing machine gun in port wing and one 0.303in Vickers 'K' machine gun in dorsal turret. Bomb load = 1,000lb. The Mk IF's forward-firing armament was augmented by four Browning 0.303in machine guns in a gun pack fitted below the fuselage. (Blenheim IVs and Vs were fitted with two Browning 0.303in machine guns in the turret, and some Blenheims were also fitted with gun pods under the nose containing a rearward-firing machine gun. Blenheims flown in Finland were armed with a Finnish L-33/34 machine gun fitted with a Vickers VGO reflector sight. Other field modifications to RAF Blenheims were made to fit cannon.)	

Appendix 2

Blenheim production list

Mark	Serials	Manufacturer
UK		
I	K7033–K7182*a	Bristol
I	L1097–L1546*b	Bristol
I	L4817–L4834	Bristol
I	L6594–L6843	Avro
I	L8362–L8407	Rootes
I	L8433–L8482	Rootes
I	L8500–L8549	Rootes
I	L8562–L8701	Rootes
I	L8597–L8632	Rootes
I	L8714–L8731	Rootes
IV	L4835–L4902	Bristol
IV	L8732–L8761	Rootes
IV	L8776–L8800	Rootes
IV	L8827–L8876	Rootes

Mark	Serials	Manufacturer
IV	L9020–L9044	Rootes
IV	L9170–L9218*c	Rootes
IV	L9237–L9273*c	Rootes
IV	L9294–L9342	Rootes
IV	L9375–L9422	Rootes
IV	L9446–L9842	Rootes
IV	N3522–N3545	Avro
IV	N3551–N3575	Avro
IV	N3578–N3604	Avro
IV	N3608–N3631	Avro
IV	N6140–N6174	Bristol
IV	N6176–N6220	Bristol
IV	N6223–N6242	Bristol
IV	P4825–P4864	Bristol
IV	P4898–P4927	Bristol

BELOW Blenheim Mk Is under licence-built construction at the Valtion Lentokonetehdas factory, Tampere, Finland, on 12 August 1941. *(SA-Kuva)*

ABOVE An early production scene from Bristol's Filton factory showing some of the first 450 Blenheim Mk Is under construction. Production of this batch began in March 1936 with deliveries of completed aircraft running from February 1938 to March 1939. *(Bristol)*

Mark	Serials	Manufacturer
IV	P6885–P6934	Bristol
IV	P6950–P6961	Bristol
IV	R2770–R2799	Avro
IV	R3590–R3639	Rootes
IV	R3660–R3709	Rootes
IV	R3730–R3779	Rootes
IV	R3800–R3849	Rootes
IV	R3870–R3919	Rootes
IV	T1792–T1832	Rootes
IV	T1848–T1897	Rootes
IV	T1921–T1960	Rootes
IV	T1985–T2004	Rootes

RIGHT A female construction worker in the cockpit of a Bristol Bolingbroke at the Fairchild aircraft factory, Longueuil, Quebec, Canada. *(Library and Archives Canada)*

Mark	Serials	Manufacturer
IV	T2031–T2080	Rootes
IV	T2112–T2141	Rootes
IV	T2161–T2190	Rootes
IV	T2216–T2255	Rootes
IV	T2273–T2292	Rootes
IV	T2318–T2357	Rootes
IV	T2381–T2400	Rootes
IV	T2425–T2444	Rootes
IV	V5370–V5399	Rootes
IV	V5420–V5469	Rootes
IV	V5490–V5539	Rootes
IV	V5560–V5599	Rootes
IV	V5620–V5659	Rootes
IV	V5680–V5699	Rootes
IV	V5720–V5769	Rootes
IV	V5790–V5829	Rootes
IV	V5850–V5899	Rootes
IV	V5920–V5969	Rootes
IV	V5990–V6039	Rootes
IV	V6060–V6099	Rootes
IV	V6120–V6149	Rootes
IV	V6170–V6199	Rootes
IV	V6220–V6269	Rootes
IV	V6290–V6339	Rootes
IV	V6360–V6399	Rootes
IV	V6420–V6469	Rootes
IV	V6490–V6529	Rootes
IV	Z5721–Z5770	Avro
IV	Z5794–Z5818	Avro
IV	Z5860–Z5909	Avro
IV	Z5947–Z5991	Avro
IV	Z6021–Z6050	Avro
IV	Z6070–Z6104	Avro
IV	Z6144–Z6193	Avro
IV	Z6239–Z6283	Avro
IV	Z6333–Z6382	Avro
IV	Z6416–Z6455	Avro
IV	Z7271–Z7320	Rootes
IV	Z7340–Z7374	Rootes
IV	Z7406–Z7455	Rootes
IV	Z7483–Z7522	Rootes
IV	Z7577–Z7569	Rootes
IV	Z7610–Z7654	Rootes
IV	Z7678–Z7712	Rootes
IV	Z7754–Z7803	Rootes
IV	Z7841–Z7860	Rootes
IV	Z7879–Z7929	Rootes
IV	Z7958–Z7992	Rootes
IV	Z9533–Z9552	Avro

FAR LEFT A wartime Canadian poster promoting the construction of Bolingbrokes, illustrated with a somewhat stylised depiction of the aircraft. *(Library and Archives Canada)*

LEFT Blenheim production being carried out at the Valtion Lentokonetehdas factory, Tampere, Finland, 12 August 1941, viewed from inside the bare shell of a Mk I nose. *(SA-Kuva)*

Mark	Serials	Manufacturer
IV	Z9572–Z9621	Avro
IV	Z9647–Z9681	Avro
IV	Z9706–Z9755	Avro
IV	Z9792–Z9836	Avro
IV	AE449–AE453	Avro
V	AD657*d	Bristol
V	AD661*d	Bristol
V	AZ851–AZ905	Rootes
V	AZ922–AZ971	Rootes
V	AZ984–AZ999	Rootes
V	BA100–BA172	Rootes
V	BA191–BA215	Rootes
V	BA228–BA262	Rootes
V	BA287–BA336	Rootes
V	BA365–BA409	Rootes
V	BA424–BA458	Rootes
V	BA471–BA505	Rootes
V	BA522–BA546	Rootes
V	BA575–BA624	Rootes
V	BA647–BA691	Rootes
V	BA708–BA757	Rootes
V	BA780–BA829	Rootes
V	BA844–BA888	Rootes
V	BA907–BA951	Rootes
V	BA978–BA999	Rootes
V	BB100–BB102	Rootes
V	BB135–BB184	Rootes
V	DJ702*e	Rootes
V	DJ707*e	Rootes
V	EH310–EH355	Rootes
V	EH371–EH420	Rootes
V	EH438–EH474	Rootes
V	EH491–EH517	Rootes

Mark	Serials	Manufacturer
Overseas		
I	BL146–BL190*f	Valtion Lentokonetehdas
IV	BL196–BL205*f	Valtion Lentokonetehdas
I	16 built*g	Ikaus AD
I	702–719*h	Fairchild
IV	9001–9004*h	Fairchild
IV	9006–9009*h	Fairchild
IV	9024–9073*h	Fairchild
IV	9075–9201*h	Fairchild
IV-W	9005*h	Fairchild
IV-W	9010–9023*h	Fairchild
IV-C	9074*h	Fairchild
IV-T	9851–10256*h*i	Fairchild

Manufacturers
A.V. Roe, Chadderton, Lancashire.
Bristol Aeroplane Co. Ltd, Filton, Bristol.
Fairchild Aircraft Ltd, Longueuil, Quebec, Canada.
Ikaus AD, Belgrade, Yugoslavia.
Rootes Securities Ltd, Speke, Liverpool and Blythe Bridge, Staffordshire.
Valtion Lentokonetehdas, Tampere, Finland.

Notes
*a K7033 was the prototype Mk I. K7072 became the prototype Mk IV.
*b Mk I L1431 was re-serialled as AX683 on return to the RAF from the SAAF.
*c Originally built as Mk Is, but converted to Mk IVs.
*d Bisley/Mk V prototypes.
*e Prototypes built to Spec B6/40.
*f Built in Finland. Five more not completed.
*g Built in Yugoslavia. Another 24 were destroyed before completion.
*h Built in Canada as Bolingbrokes.
*i Plus 51 spare airframes.

Appendix 3

RAF Blenheim squadrons

Mk I	
Home bomber	Nos 18, 21, 34, 44, 57, 61, 62, 82, 90, 101, 104, 107, 108, 110, 114, 139 and 144.
Home fighter	Nos 23, 25, 29, 64, 68, 92, 141, 145, 219, 222, 229, 234, 235, 236, 242, 245, 248, 600, 601 and 604.
Overseas bomber	Nos 8, 11, 20, 30, 34, 39, 45, 55, 60, 62, 84, 113 and 211.
Overseas fighter	Nos 27, 30 and 203.
Mk IV	
Bomber Command	Nos 15, 18, 21, 34, 35, 40, 57, 82, 88, 90, 101, 104, 107, 108, 110, 114, 139, 218, 226, 500 and 608.
Middle East	Nos 8, 11, 14, 45, 52, 55, 84, 104, 105, 107, 113, 162, 203, 223, 244 and 614.
Army Co-operation	Nos 13, 53, 59, and 614.
Far East bomber	No 34.
Coastal Command fighter	Nos 143, 234, 235, 236, 248, 252, 254, 272, 404 and 614.
Coastal Command bomber	Nos 53, 59 and 86.
Fighter Command	Nos 248 and 600.
Overseas fighter	No 60.
Mk V	
Middle East	Nos 8, 13, 18, 114, 244, 454 and 614.
Far East	Nos 42, 113 and 211.

Note: Blenheims also served with the Royal Navy Fleet Air Arm, plus some units of the RAAF, RCAF, RNZAF and SAAF under RAF control.

RIGHT The 'Blenheim Boys' of 101 Squadron pictured outside Weasenham Hall, Norfolk, in January 1941. At the time the unit was based at RAF West Raynham, and the stately home was taken over to accommodate flying personnel to disperse them away from the base from 9 November 1940. *(101 Squadron Archives)*

Squadron codes		
Squadron	**Pre-war**	**Wartime**
8	–	HV-
11	OY-	EX-
13	AN-	OO-
14	BF-	CX-
15	–	LS-
18	GU-	WV-
20	–	HN-
21	JP-	YH-
23	MS-	YP-
25	RX-	ZK-
27	–	EG-
29	YB-	RO-
30	DP-	VT-
34	LB-	EG-
35	–	TL-
39	–	XZ-
40	–	BL-
42	–	AW-
44	JW-	KM-
45	–	OB-
52	–	–
53	TE-	PZ-
55	GM-	–
57	EQ-	DX-
59	PJ-	TR-
60	AD-	MU-
61	LS-	QR-
62	JO-	PT-
64	XQ-	SH-
68	–	WM-
82	OZ-	UX-
84	UR-	PY-
86	–	BX-
88	–	RH-
90	TW-	WP-
92	–	GR-
101	LU-	SR-
104	PO-	EP-
105	–	GB-
107	BZ-	OM-
108	MF-	LD-
110	AY-	VE-
113	BT-	AD-
114	FD-	RT-
139	SY-	XD-
140	–	ZW-
141	–	TW-
143	–	HO-
144	–	PL-
145	–	SO-
162	–	GK-
173	–	–
203	–	CJ-, NT-
211	LJ-	UQ-

212	–	DB-
218	–	HA-
219	–	FK-
222	–	ZD-
223	–	AO-
226	–	MQ-
229	–	RE-
233	–	ZS-
234	–	AZ-
235	–	LA-
236	–	FA-
242	–	LE-
244	–	–
245	–	DX-
248	–	WR-
252	–	PN-
254	–	QY-
272	–	XK-
285	–	VG-
287	–	KZ-
288	–	RP-
289	–	YE-
404	–	EE-
406	–	HU-
407	–	RR-
415	–	GX-
454	–	–
489	–	XA-
500	–	MK-
516	–	–
521	–	5O
526	–	MD-
527	–	WN-
528	–	–
600	MV-	BQ-
601	YN-	UF-
604	WQ-	NG-
608	–	UL-
614	–	LJ-

ABOVE Blenheim Mk IVs of 82 Squadron at their base at RAF Watton in Suffolk. The unit suffered heavy losses during the Battle of France, especially during a raid on Gembloux on 17 May 1940, during which all 12 of the Blenheims despatched failed to return to base. However, the unit recovered to fly raids on invasion barges in the Channel ports during the Battle of Britain. *(Air Ministry)*

Appendix 4

The Blenheim family tree

Bristol Type 135

A small, twin-engined, low-wing monoplane able to carry two crew and six passengers at high speed. It was originally intended to be powered by two Bristol Aquila engines, but these were later substituted with a pair of Bristol Mercury engines and the aircraft was redesignated as the Bristol Type 142.

Bristol Type 142

Ordered by Lord Rothermere of the *Daily Mail* and named 'Britain First', this was a development of the proposed Type 135. Powered by two Bristol Mercury VIS 2 engines, it first flew from Filton on 12 April 1935. Given the civil registration G-ADCZ, Lord Rothermere

donated it to the nation for military development and it gained the experimental registration R-12 before being given the military serial K7557. It was used for military trials and for the familiarisation of RAF pilots scheduled to convert to the Blenheim when the type became available. 'Britain First' later became an instructional airframe, was damaged during an enemy bombing raid and this historic airframe was sadly scrapped in 1944.

Bristol Type 143

An enlarged version of the Type 142, powered by two Bristol Aquila engines and able to carry eight passengers. It was completed during early 1935 and given the civil registration G-ADEK.

RIGHT Bristol Type 142 K7557 'Britain First'.
(© Andy Hay/Flyingart)

RIGHT Bristol Type 143 G-ADEK, wearing its R-14 experimental registration.
(© Andy Hay/Flyingart)

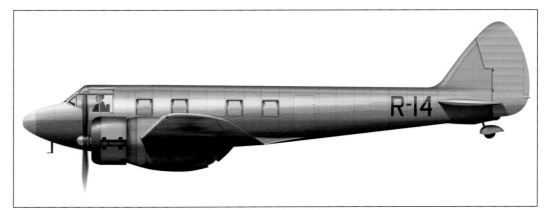

Delays with the production of the Aquila engine meant that it did not fly until 20 January 1936. It gained the experimental registration R-14, but remained at Filton as a test-bed for the unsuccessful development of the Aquila, which was cancelled in 1938. The Type 143 was scrapped in 1940.

Bristol Type 143F

Finland had shown interest in a military version of the Type 143, though only if it could be fitted with Mercury engines. Designated the Type 143F, the design looked at introducing armament and an order was submitted for nine examples. However, with the already successful Type 142M being a better option, the Finnish government looked towards that instead and the Type 143F design was abandoned.

Bristol Type 142M Blenheim Mk I

The Type 142M ('M' for Military) was a bomber development of the Type 142 'Britain First' design, and was to become the prototype Blenheim I. The main differences were in the design of the cockpit to allow for a bomb-aimer

and the necessary equipment, the movement of the wing from a low position to a mid-wing position in order to allow for the incorporation of bomb cells and the fitting of a rotating mid-dorsal turret. The design was given the Air Ministry Specification B28/35, which was submitted in August 1935 and called for the aircraft to be powered by two Mercury VIIIs. Just the following month 150 Blenheim Is were ordered straight from the drawing board and the first example, K7033, carried out its maiden flight from Filton on 25 June 1936. The third aircraft off the production line, dual-control fitted K7035, became the first Blenheim to be delivered to the RAF on 1 March 1937, when it was issued to 114 Squadron at Wyton.

Blenheim Mk IF

Originally considered for use as a long-range day-fighter in 1938, by the time of the arrival of enemy fighters such as the Messerschmitt Bf 109 the Blenheim Mk IF was instead predominantly used in the night-fighter role. Its principal difference was the fitting of a gun pack over the area of the Blenheim's bomb cells,

LEFT The prototype Bristol Type 142M K7033, the forerunner to the Blenheim Mk I. *(© Andy Hay/Flyingart)*

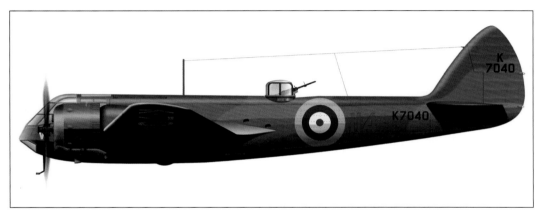

LEFT Blenheim Mk I K7040 of 114 Squadron, which was the first front-line RAF unit to receive the type on 1 March 1937 while it was based at Wyton. *(© Andy Hay/Flyingart)*

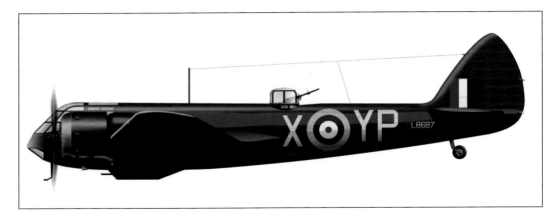

RIGHT Blenheim Mk IF
L8687/YP-X of
23 Squadron. This
night-fighter was being
flown by Squadron
Leader J. O'Brien on
the night of 18/19 June
1940, when its crew
succeeded in shooting
down a Heinkel He 111
near Six Mile Bottom
in Norfolk.
(© Andy Hay/Flyingart)

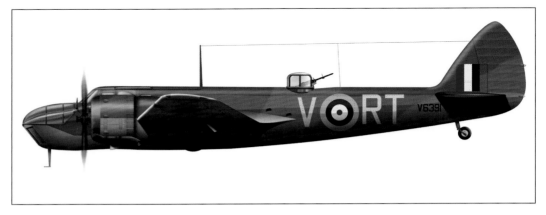

RIGHT Blenheim Mk IV
V6391/RT-V of
114 Squadron. This
aircraft was flown
by Sergeant Ivor
Broom during a
daylight raid on the
Knapsack power
station near Cologne
on 12 August 1941.
This distinguished
RAF pilot's career
continued until the
mid-1970s when
he retired as an Air
Marshal. Sir Ivor
Broom passed away
in 2003.
(© Andy Hay/Flyingart)

containing four fixed forward-firing Browning 0.303in machine guns in addition to the single gun in the port wing. Approximately 200 Mk Is were converted to Mk IF standard, the first of which arrived on the strength of 25 Squadron at Hawkinge in December 1938. Although this variant served during the Battle of Britain, by the end of 1940 it was being rapidly replaced.

Blenheim PRI

Only one Blenheim, Mk I L1348, is thought to have been modified specifically for photographic reconnaissance. The aircraft's bodywork was smoothed down and sealed and its turret and armament were all removed. It also had a pair of Rotol constant-speed propellers fitted and eventually reached 294mph at 13,000ft, making it considerably faster than its bomber brethren. However, the development of even faster Supermarine Spitfires to PR configuration made its further development redundant.

Blenheim Mk II

Only one aircraft, Mk I L1222, was fitted with long-range tanks, a strengthened undercarriage

and externally fitted bombs as an experiment to improve the Blenheim's range. The development never went into production. (Blenheim Is supplied to the Finnish Air Force were also designated as Mk IIs by Bristol.)

Blenheim Mk III

Another interim attempt to improve the Blenheim's range before the development of the Mk IV, the Mk III was of similar specification to the Mk II though without the long-range tanks being fitted. The variant was briefly designated as the Mk IV-L ('L' for Long-range), and it is thought that as many as 60-plus were modified in long-nose configuration, but it never went into production as such and instead the idea was developed as the Mk IV.

Bristol Type 149 Blenheim Mk IV

Built to Air Ministry Specification 11/36, prototype K7072 was initially called the Bolingbroke Mk I and featured a lengthened nose of similar profile to the Blenheim Mk I. Powered by Mercury XV engines, it carried out its maiden flight on 24 September 1937, and

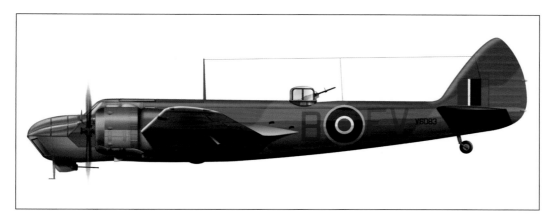

LEFT **Blenheim Mk IV V6083/FV-B of 13 Operational Training Unit is depicted fitted with a rearward-firing machine gun in an under-nose turret.**
(© Andy Hay/Flyingart)

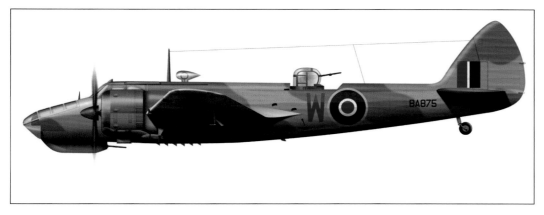

LEFT **Blenheim Mk V BA875/W of 18 Squadron. This was the aircraft flown by Wing Commander Hugh Malcolm VC on 4 December 1942, when 50-plus Messerschmitt Bf 109s set upon the small force of Blenheims he was leading. Although he and his crew were shot down and killed in this aircraft, Wing Commander Malcolm was posthumously awarded the Victoria Cross for his determination to carry out his duty on this operation, despite the overwhelming odds his bomber force faced. Only three of the nine Blenheims which attacked their target made it back to Allied lines, all crash-landing as a result of the damage they had sustained from the enemy fighters.**
(© Andy Hay/Flyingart)

complaints about the windscreen being too far away from the pilot led to the redesigned scalloped canopy. Subsequently becoming the Blenheim Mk IV, the first examples arrived with 53 Squadron at Odiham in January 1939.

Blenheim Mk IVF

Similarly fitted with a gun pack containing four Browning 0.303in machine guns as the Mk IF.

Type 160 Blenheim V

Originally called the Bisley Mk I but later renamed the Blenheim Mk V, this was a development of the type to Air Ministry Specification B6/40 aimed at improving the Blenheim's fighting capability in the advanced hostile environment at a later stage of the war. This variant was fitted with either Mercury 25 or 30 engines for increased power; however, the fitting of a heavier BX turret, more machine guns and an increased amount of armour protection for the crew led to the Blenheim V having a significantly increased operational weight. The first Bisley Mk I, AD657, flew from Filton on 24 February 1941. The variant went

through several design changes, resulting in the Mk VD, which was a tropicalised version intended to carry out operations in North Africa and the Far East and which entered service in late 1942. The Mk V proved unpopular with the aircrew who flew it and the groundcrew who maintained it. Poor performance and heavy losses saw it replaced by US-built aircraft in North Africa. The last Blenheim Mk Vs were delivered in June 1943 and the mark flew operations until April 1944.

Bolingbroke Mk I (Canadian-built)

The Bolingbroke name originally given to K7072 was revived for licence-built Blenheim Mk IVs constructed by the Fairchild Aircraft Company Ltd at Longueuil, Quebec, Canada. Fitted with imported parts and Mercury VIII engines, the first example, 702, flew on 14 September 1939.

Bolingbroke Mk II

The fifth Bolingbroke Mk I was fitted out with US equipment and built to American standards. This modification was initially called the Bolingbroke Mk II, but all later aircraft built similarly were known as Bolingbroke Mk IVs.

Bolingbroke Mk III

Just one Bolingbroke, 717, was experimentally fitted with Edo floats and became the sole Mk III. The trials were not a great success and the aircraft was later fitted with a conventional undercarriage.

Bolingbroke Mk IV

As mentioned above for the Mk II, aircraft fitted with US equipment and built to American standards were designated Bolingbroke Mk IVs. Deliveries of this variant to the RCAF began from January 1941.

Bolingbroke Mk IV-C

Only one example, 9074, was fitted with 900hp Wright Cyclone R-1820 engines to become the sole Bolingbroke Mk IV-C.

Bolingbroke Mk IV-W

A batch of 15 Bolingbrokes were fitted with

825hp Pratt & Whitney SB43G Twin Wasp Junior engines, becoming Mk IV-Ws. However, performance was not improved and Fairchild reverted back to fitting Bristol Mercury engines to the Bolingbroke.

Bolingbroke Mk IV-T

Basic Bolingbroke Mk IVs fitted with Mercury XX engines were designated the Mk IV-T. These were built in their hundreds and used a general-purpose training aircraft, none being lost in action. It is this variant which survived in numbers and has provided the basis for the majority of preserved examples and surviving parts. (G-BPIV now comprises a Bolingbroke Mk IV-T airframe with a restored Blenheim Mk I nose now fitted to it instead of its former Bolingbroke Mk IV nose.)

Bolingbroke Mk IV-TT

Bolingbroke Mk IV-Ts fitted with winching gear in the rear fuselage and a drogue in the bomb bay were designated as the Mk IV-TT for target-towing duties.

BELOW Bolingbroke Mk III 717 fitted with Edo floats. This was the only example fitted with floats, but the trial was not a success as the engines ingested too much water on take-off. (RCAF)

Appendix 5

Foreign service

Canada

While some RCAF units flew Blenheims on active service with the RAF, hundreds were licence-built in Canada and flown on various duties there, so warrant inclusion in this appendix covering the type's service with 'foreign' countries.

Canada was the main overseas user of the Blenheim, built locally by Fairchild under licence and called the Bolingbroke. The type was used in various roles, from a general training aircraft to being sent operationally to the west coast of North America after Japan had entered the war, some aircraft being fitted with fighter gun packs. Two RCAF squadrons flew anti-submarine patrols from the Aleutian Islands from June 1942 to December 1943. A Bolingbroke from 115 Squadron flown by Flight Sergeant P. Thomas was the first RCAF aircraft to sink a Japanese submarine on 7 July 1942. Other squadrons operated from the eastern seaboard protecting Canada.

However, the Bolingbroke was a vital training aircraft as part of the Empire Air Training Scheme, where thousands of pilots, navigators and air gunners were able to train in safer skies than those available in the UK. The type was also used for target-towing duties and for surveys and patrols over the wide expanses of the Canadian terrain until well after the war had ended.

BELOW Finnish Blenheim Mk I BL-115 comes in to land at Luonetjärvi in late March 1944. *(SA-Kuva)*

RIGHT Bolingbroke Mk IV-T 9140/P of 115 (Bomber Reconnaissance) Squadron RCAF.
(© Andy Hay/Flyingart)

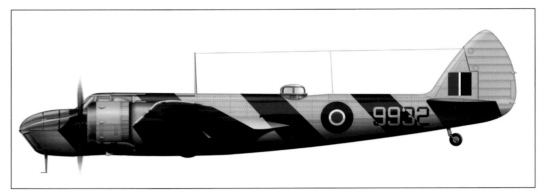

RIGHT RCAF Bolingbroke Mk IV-TT 9932 wearing the high-visibility black and yellow paint scheme applied to the Service's target-tugs during the Second World War.
(© Andy Hay/Flyingart)

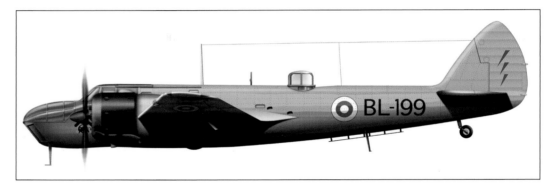

RIGHT It was Mk IV BL-199, having by then lost its wartime camouflage, that had the honour of flying the last Finnish Air Force Blenheim sortie on 20 May 1958.
(© Andy Hay/Flyingart)

Croatia

The Croatian Air Force operated 12 ex-Yugoslav Mk Is, which the Germans passed on to them after their invasion of Yugoslavia. These Blenheims were used against the Russians.

Finland

The first foreign country to import the Blenheim was Finland, which then began to licence-build the type before the Second World War began. Finnish Blenheims were in action against the Russians during the Winter War which began in November 1939, until Finland surrendered in March 1940. When German forces invaded Russia in June 1941, the Finns unwittingly found themselves as allies of the Germans. Production of the Blenheim

Mk I and Mk IV continued at Tampere and the new aircraft, along with the survivors of the Winter War, were later in action against the Russians in the Continuation War until the ceasefire on the Finnish front in September 1944. Some of the few surviving Finnish Blenheims continued to fly on aerial survey work after the war, with the last sortie taking place as late as 20 May 1958.

Free French

Several Free French units flew Blenheim Mk IVs and Vs in the Western Desert, Syria and Tunisia from 1941 until August 1945. At one point in the war the Free French Group Lorraine's Blenheim Mk IVs and Vs operated against Vichy French forces in Senegal.

LEFT Blenheim Mk IV N3522/4 of the Free French Group Lorraine depicted wearing the cross of Lorraine roundels and a three-colour rudder applied to its desert camouflage scheme. (© Andy Hay/Flyingart)

LEFT Blenheim Mk I 160 of the Royal Yugoslavian Air Force in an all-over silver paint scheme. (© Andy Hay/Flyingart)

Greece

Blenheim Mk IVs and Vs served with 13 Squadron of the Royal Hellenic Air Force from October 1942 until October 1943, but their numbers were decimated firstly by the Regia Aeronautica and then the Luftwaffe.

Portugal

Portugal inherited its first 12 Blenheims as a result of aircraft which had forced-landed in this neutral country en route to Gibraltar. Another batch was supplied as part-payment for the Allied use of bases on the Azores, west of Portugal in the Atlantic. Some of the Portuguese Blenheims continued flying until 1949.

Romania

A total of 52 Blenheims were supplied to Romania just prior to and in the early stages of the Second World War. This was an attempt to keep the country on the Allied side, but it joined the Axis powers. The Romanian Blenheims flew under Luftwaffe control in action against the Russians and are known to have been in use up until October 1944, by which time losses and a lack of spares availability saw them become obsolete.

South Africa

In early 1939 Blenheim Mk I L1431 was sent to South Africa and was test-flown from Cape Town on 11 March. The South Africans liked the aircraft as part of its defence expansion plan, so orders were submitted though no further deliveries took place. The Blenheim remained with the SAAF until 29 August 1940, whereupon it returned to the UK and was re-serialled as AX683.

Turkey

The Turkish Air Force was supplied with 63 Blenheims, comprising examples of all three marks. Deliveries were split between dates spanning from just before the war, by which time 30 Blenheims had arrived, up to 1943. The country kept out of the war and continued to operate Blenheims until 1948.

Yugoslavia

Before the war 20 Avro-built Blenheim Mk Is were exported to Yugoslavia and then a further 16 were licence-built at Zenum. They suffered heavy losses during the German invasion and the survivors were passed on to Croatia.

Appendix 6

Glossary and abbreviations

A&AEE Aircraft & Armaments Experimental Establishment

AASF Advanced Air Striking Force

AFDU Air Fighting Development Unit

AI Airborne Intercept or Interception radar (used by night-fighters to home-in on targets)

AP Air Publication (an official manual containing the information required to fly and maintain an aircraft)

ARC Aircraft Restoration Company

ASI Airspeed indicator

BAe British Aerospace

Bf An abbreviation for Bayerische Flugzeugwerke AG, the company which designed the Bf 109 but later changed its name to Messerschmitt (hence Bf 109, not Me 109)

Boost The amount of additional pressure created by a supercharger

CofG Centre of gravity

Feathering Turning the propeller blades of a stopped engine edge-on to the airflow to reduce drag

FOD Foreign object damage

GP General-purpose bomb

HC High-capacity bomb

hp Horsepower – the measurement used to denote the power of an engine

IAS Indicated airspeed

IFF Identification friend or foe

IFR Instrument flight rules

MU Maintenance Unit (RAF)

NDT Non-destructive testing

NOTAM Notice to airmen. Advisory notice giving information on the establishment, condition or change in any aeronautical facility, service, procedure or hazard

OC Officer Commanding

OTU Operational Training Unit

psi Pounds per square inch (lb/in^2) – a measurement of pressure

RAAF Royal Australian Air Force

RAE Royal Aircraft Establishment

RAF Royal Air Force

RCAF Royal Canadian Air Force

RNZAF Royal New Zealand Air Force

rpg Rounds per gun

rpm Revolutions per minute

R/T Radio telegraphy – sending voice messages over a radio

SAAF South African Air Force

SBC Small-bomb container

SSI Structurally significant item

Supercharger A device to increase the inlet pressure of a piston engine to boost its power

SWG Standard wire gauge

Trimming tab A small additional control surface on the trailing edge of an aileron, rudder or elevator that can be adjusted to aid the stability of an aircraft at different weights of intended flight regimes

UHF Ultra-high frequency (radio), in the wavelengths 225–400MHz (mainly used for military aircraft communications)

UK United Kingdom

US United States

VFR Visual Flight Rules

VHF Very high frequency (radio), in the wavelengths 118–136MHz

W/T Wireless telegraphy – sending Morse code messages by radio

Appendix 7

Useful contacts

Aircraft Restoration Company/ Historic Flying Ltd
Building 425, Duxford airfield, Duxford,
Cambridge, CB2 4QR, UK
Tel: +44 (0)1223 835313
Fax: +44 (0)1223 837290
E-mail: admin@arc-duxford.co.uk
Website: www.arc-duxford.co.uk

The Blenheim Society
Hon Treasurer Ron Scott
25 Herongate Road
Cheshunt, Herts
EN8 0TU
Tel: 01992 442608
e-mail: r.j.scott@ntlworld.co.uk
Website: www.blenheimsociety.org.uk

Dunlop Tyres
40 Fort Parkway
Erdington
Birmingham
West Midlands
B24 9HL
Tel: 0121 384 8800
www.dunlopaircrafttyres.com

Bibliography

Air Publication 1464A, *RAF Engineering Manual: General Principles, Volume 1* (Air Ministry, 1940)

Air Publication 1464B, *RAF Engineering Manual: General Principles, Volume 1* (Air Ministry, 1942)

Air Publication 1491D, *Bristol Mercury Mk 15, 20, 25, 26, 30, 31 & 32 Aero-Engines* (Air Ministry, 1950)

Air Publication 1530A Volume I, *The Blenheim I Aeroplane (Day-Bombing Landplane)* (Air Ministry, December 1938)

Air Publication 1530A, *Pilot's Notes Blenheim I Aeroplane* (Air Ministry, April 1939)

Air Publication 1530B Volume I, *The Blenheim IV Aeroplane* (Air Ministry, September 1939)

Air Publication 1538, *Propellers: General Information* (Air Ministry, 1967)

Air Publication 1659B Volume I, *Bristol Gun Turrets* (Air Ministry, June 1940)

Air Publication 1870B, *Notes on Fighting and Defensive Tactics for Bomber Aircraft (Blenheim)* (Air Ministry, June 1940)

Bomber Command – The Air Ministry's Account of Bomber Command's Offensive Against the Axis, September 1939–July 1941 (Air Ministry, 1941)

Bowyer, Chaz, *Bristol Blenheim* (Ian Allan, 1984)

Churchill, Winston S., *The Second World War Volume II – Their Finest Hour* (Cassell & Co., 1949)

Edwards, Richard and Edwards, Peter J., *Heroes and Landmarks of British Aviation* (Pen & Sword, 2012)

Flintham, Vic and Thomas, Andrew, *Combat Codes* (Airlife Publishing, 2003)

Grey, C.G., 'Britain First' (*The Aeroplane*, 21 August 1935)

Halley, James J., *The Squadrons of the Royal Air Force* (Air-Britain Historians Ltd, 1980)

Jefford, Wing Commander C.G., *RAF Squadrons* (Airlife Publishing, 1998)

Mason, Francis K., *The British Fighter Since 1912* (Putnam, 1992)

Mason, Francis K., *The British Bomber Since 1914* (Putnam, 1994)

Middlebrook, Martin and Everitt, Chris, *The Bomber Command War Diaries – An Operational Reference Book 1939–1945* (Midland Publishing, 2011)

Orange, Vincent, *Churchill and his Airmen* (Grub Street, 2013)

Richards, Denis, *Royal Air Force 1939–45 Vol II – The Fight Avails* (Her Majesty's Stationery Office, 1954)

Richards, Denis and Saunders, Hilary St G., *Royal Air Force 1939–45 Vol I – The Fight at Odds* (Her Majesty's Stationery Office, 1953)

Robertson, Bruce, *British Military Aircraft Serials 1911–1971* (Ian Allan, 1964)

Saunders, Hilary St G., *Royal Air Force 1939–45 Vol III – The Fight is Won* (Her Majesty's Stationery Office, 1954)

The Battle of Britain August–October 1940 (Ministry of Information, 1941)

Thetford, Owen, *Aircraft of the Royal Air Force Since 1918* (Putnam, 1979)

Warner, Graham, *The Bristol Blenheim – A Complete History* (Crécy Publishing, 2002)

Index

A&AEE Martlesham Heath 8, 20-22, 24
Advertisements 19, 22-23, 31, 157
Aero engine types
    Bristol Aquila 18-19, 21-22, 160-161
    Bristol Mercury 18, 43, 49-50, 60, 84,
      99, 160-161, 164; VI S.2 19, 160;
      VIII 22; XV 162; XX 45, 49-50, 57,
      83, 164; 25/30 163
    Pratt & Whitney SB43G Twin
      Wasp 164
    Rolls-Royce Merlin 14
    Wright Cyclone R-1820 164
Aeroplane, The magazine 20
Air Council 20
Aircraft Restoration Company (ARC)
    (Propshop Ltd) 9, 12-15, 41-42, 44,
    46, 48-49, 53-55, 60, 72, 96, 130-
    132, 169
    Ministry of Defence (MoD) contracts
      13-14
Aircrew 60, 101, 110.149
    access 96, 106-107
    brevets 108
    briefing/debriefing 98, 123, 127
Air Ministry 18-20, 25-26, 57
    Specification B6/40 163
    Specification 11/36 24, 162
    Specification B28/35 20, 161
Air Publications 132
    *Notes on Fighting and Defence Tactics
      for Bomber Aircraft (Blenheim)* 114
    Pilot's Notes 101, 103
Armament 91-93, 154
    bomb loads and loading 91-93 144-
      148
    Browning 0.303in machine gun 27, 52,
      66, 68, 70, 72-74, 90-91, 147, 162
    depth charges 150
    flares 148
    gun pack 27, 52, 69-70, 163, 165
    gun turrets 22, 28, 61, 66-68, 89, 91,
      98, 106-107, 121, 147, 150, 163
    Hispano 20mm cannon 36
    Lewis gun 28, 91
    practice bombs 148
    RAE containers 147
    small bomb containers (SBCs) 146
    Vickers machine gun 147
    250lb bombs 33, 92-93, 144, 146-147
    500lb bombs 92-93, 144-145, 147
Ashfield, Flg Off G. 28
Auchinleck, Gen 36
Avro 53, 133, 157, 167
    Lancaster 8, 13, 30, 44

Ballast weights 134
Barnwell, Capt Frank 18, 20-21, 24, 57
Barratt, AVM Sir Arthur Sheridan 25
Battle for Malta 36
Battle of Britain 28-30, 45, 159, 162
Battle of Britain film 46
Battle of France 26, 159
Baxter, Raymond 41
Beaverbrook, Lord 19
Blenheim Boys 8, 11, 44, 101, 130,
    158, 173
Blenheim (Duxford) Ltd 44, 133
Blenheim Society 129, 132-133, 169
Bomb compartments and doors 67-70,
    72
Bombing tactics 114-121
    approach phase 114

avoidance of anti-aircraft fire 118, 120
    defensive manoeuvres 115
      at night 118
      avoiding action 119-121
    fighters 120-121
    fighting control 117
    leading air gunner 118
    low flying 117
    over clouds 118
    searchlights 119
    the attack 114-115
    visibility 120
Bos, Karel 13
Boscombe Down 22
Boulton Paul Overstrand 20-22
Bristol Aeroplane Co. 18, 21, 157
    Bombay 32
    F.2b Fighter 18
    Freighter 20
    Scout F 20
    Type No 135 18, 160
    Type No 142 'Britain First' 18-22, 57,
      160
    Type 143 19-22, 160-161
    Type 143F 161
    Type 149 Bolingbroke Mks I, II, III, IV,
      IV-C, IV-W, IV-T and IV-TT (see also
      Fairchild) 24, 42-43, 163-166
Bristol Blenheim marks
    Mk I Prototype (Type 142M) 17, 19-20,
      22, 161
    Mk I 5, 7-8, 22-24, 31, 33-34, 38, 41,
      44-47, 52, 57, 61, 63, 95, 103-105,
      107, 112, 131, 133, 146, 152-158,
      161-162, 165-167, 173
    Mk IF night fighter 8, 27-29, 45, 52,
      69-70, 117, 161-162
    Mk II 162
    Mk III 162
    Mk IV (Type 149) Prototype 24, 162
    Mk IV 9-10, 25-26, 30-31, 33, 37-39,
      45, 52, 63, 101, 111-112, 121, 132,
      146-148, 158-159, 162-163, 166-
      167, 173
    Mk IVF 27, 35, 163
    Mk V (Type 160) 'Bisley' 37-39, 122-127,
      129, 138, 149-151, 158, 166-167
    Mk VD 163
    PRI 162
Bristol Evening World 18
British Civil Airworthiness Requirements
    (BCAR) 45-46
British Expeditionary Force (BEF) 9, 25
Broom, AM Sir Ivor 101, 116, 162
Builder's plate 53

Cameras and mountings 67-69, 89, 124
Checks
    airborne 98
    landing 99
    start-up 97, 104
    pre take-off 98, 105-106
Churchill, Winston 16
Civil Aviation Authority (CAA)
    Airworthiness Approval Note (AAN)
      45-46
Cockpit 47-48, 52, 60, 63, 79-83, 99,
    101, 156
    access 61, 63, 102
    air-intake shutter controls 88
    carburettor cut-out controls 88
    control column 79-80

control handwheel 79, 81, 117, 144
    dual controls 80-81
    emergency exit 66, 111
    engine controls 47, 52, 60, 63, 87-88,
      142, 144
    flying controls 48-49, 60, 78-83, 98,
      108, 133
    gun-firing button 117
    instrument panel 52, 65
    machine gun ring sight 91
    pilot's control chassis 60, 63, 79, 83
    propeller pitch controls 88, 97, 106
    undercarriage lamp indicators 78
    windscreen 24, 163
Collishaw, Air Cdre Raymond 32-33, 36
Colour schemes 9, 22, 49-50, 52,
    166-167
Coningham, AVM Arthur 36
Crashes and losses 9, 23-26, 28-30,
    32-38, 42-43, 45, 107, 116, 132-133,
    159, 163
Croatian Air Force 166-167
Cunliffe-Lister, Sir Philip 20
Cunliffe Thornton, Sgt Hector 122, 149

Daily Express 19
Daily Mail 20, 160
de Havilland Mosquito 8, 101
Denham airfield 132
Display routine 99
Dornier Do 17 28-29; Do 17Z 26
Douglas Dakota 13
Dowding, Air Marshal Sir Hugh 19
Duke-Woolley, Flt Lt Raymond 27-28
Duxford Airfield 5, 11-14, 41, 43, 46,
    48, 53

Edwards, Wg Cdr Hughie 36, 44, 112
Electric car 10, 44-45, 47, 133
Electrical system 51-52, 84, 104
    magnetos 98, 102-104, 130
    spark plugs 103
Elizabeth, Queen 26
Empire Air Training Scheme 165
Engine mountings 46, 50-51, 72-73,
    83-85
Engines 41-42, 49-50, 135, 142, 154
    change 138, 151
    cooling 84, 99
    cowl gills 84, 97-99, 106-107, 110,
      142-143
    cylinder heads 43, 50, 84, 97, 131,
      151
    exhaust system 84
    nacelles 48-49, 71, 74, 83-84, 89
    pistons 50, 84, 131
    priming 96,102, 104
    start-up 96-97, 102, 104-105
    tests 102-103
    warm-up 102
Entry into RAF service 17, 23, 25,
    161-163
    service evaluation trials 22

Fairchild Bolingbroke 45-46, 52, 106-
    107, 130, 156
    Mk I 45
    Mk IV-T 45, 132-133
Fairey Battle 25-26
Filton 8, 21, 156, 160-161, 163
Finnish Air Force 134, 146, 162, 165-166
    Luonetjärvi airfield 131, 165

Flying 108-109
    approach and landing 99, 109-110
      drill of vital actions 110
      touching down 110
    climbing 107
    cruising 107-108
    general handling 98-99
Flying clothing 101-102, 124, 149
Flying control surfaces 49, 137, 153
Free French Group 166-167
Fuel system and tanks 24, 46, 51-52,
    72, 83-85, 97-99, 104, 131, 133, 148,
    154, 162
    auxiliary tank 36
    carburettors 31, 84, 88-89, 97, 99, 142
    consumption 108
    jettison valve 89
    tropical filters 31
Fuselage 22, 26, 43-44, 48, 52, 54,
    60-61, 69, 133-134
    access to main cabin 67
    centre section 42, 133, 135
    front section 61, 135
    nose section 7-8, 10-11, 24, 44-48,
      52, 63, 66, 109, 157, 162, 164
    rear 46, 60, 66-70, 98, 164
    skin panelling and riveting 47, 60, 67
    stern frame 60-61, 70-71

Geary, Plt Off A.C. 107
George VI, HM King 26
German Afrika Korps 34, 36-37
Gloster Gladiator 20
Goode, Sqn Ldr George 37
Gordon-Finlayson, Sqn Ldr J.R. 107
Graziani, Marshal 33
Groundcrew 25, 39, 97, 102, 104, 127,
    130, 142, 146, 163
    armourers 146-147
    engineering officers 151
    fabric worker 151
    fitters 129
    instrument mechanic 150
    riggers 26, 137

Hamilton-Brookes, Sqn Ldr Hugh 23
Handley Page
    Halifax 30
    Hampden 25
Harris, AM Sir Arthur Travers 30-31
Hawker
    Audax 23
    Hardy 31
    Hind 23, 32
    Hurricanes 13-14, 26-29, 33, 39, 54
Haydon-Baillie, Ormond 42-43
Heinkel
    He 59 28-29
    He 111 27-29, 162
Hendon RAF Displays 19, 21, 23
Historic Flying Ltd (HFL) 12-13, 15
Hogg, Plt Off D.W. 29
Hydraulic system 8, 23, 51-52, 71, 74,
    76, 83, 89, 97-99, 106, 140-141

Imperial Japanese Army Air Force 39
Imperial War Museum (IWM) Duxford 11,
    13, 42-43, 46, 132
Inspection panels 144, 151

Jacking and lifting points 134-137
Junkers Ju 88 28-29

Kato, Lt Col Tateo 39
Kells, Plt Off Peter 27
Krantz, Aircraftman R. 142

Larcombe, John 43
Lewis, Robert T. 18
Leyland, RO Sgt R.H. 28
Lockheed
    Ventura 38
    12 Electra 19
Longmore, ACM Sir Arthur 32-34
Lubrication 143-144
Luftwaffe 27, 30, 35, 38, 167

Maiden flights 19-22, 24, 43-44, 57, 163
Maintenance and servicing 146, 148-151
Malcolm, Wg Cdr Hugh 38, 112, 163
Markings 20, 44, 167
McFarlane, Corp H.B. 142
McLuckie, Flt Sgt 'Jock' 39
McPherson Flg Off Andrew 25
Messerschmitt
    Bf 109 23, 27, 35, 38, 98, 115, 161, 163
    Me 110 115
Mitsubishi A6M Zero 39
Morris, Observer Plt Off G.E. 28
Munich Crisis 23

Nakajima Ki-43 39
Navigators/bomb aimers 24, 63, 66, 79, 99, 109, 111, 123-124, 127, 165
Nelson, Ralph 10, 45

O'Brien, Sqn Ldr Joseph 28, 162
O'Connor, Gen Richard 34
Oil system 51, 83-87, 97-98, 103, 105, 106, 131, 137, 140
Olmstead, LAC K. 137
Operation Crusader 36
Operation Dynamo, Dunkirk evacuation 26-27, 30
Operation Millennium 30
Operation Torch 37
Oxygen apparatus 93

Parachute drill 111
    abandon aircraft order 111
Paris Show 21
Pegg, Test Pilot Bill 24
Performance 17-22, 27-28, 154, 163
    range and fuel economy 108, 154, 162
Permit to Fly 46
Phoney War 26
Pipe, Dave 55
Pneumatic system 51, 89-91, 97, 141-142
Portuguese Air Force 167
Prins, François 116
Production 23, 34, 155-157
    export sales 24, 34, 165-167
    licence building: Canada (Fairchild) 24, 42, 156-157, 163-165; Finland (Valtion) 42, 91, 131, 155, 157, 161; Yugoslavia (Ikaus) 157, 166
Propellers 19, 45, 49, 60, 85, 88, 97-99, 130, 144, 154, 162
    hub 85
    pitch 88,97, 106, 109
    spinners 22
Proudfoot, Hoof 44
Proudfoot, Lee 13
Pughe Lloyd, AVM Hugh 36

Radar 27-29
Radio/avionics 52, 97
RAF Battle of Britain Memorial Flight (BBMF) 13-14, 44
Refuelling 131, 134, 146, 151
Regia Aeronautica 167
Remanufactured components 54-55

Retro Track & Air 46, 169
Rigging 134-137
Roles
    anti-shipping 25, 30, 37, 39, 122-127, 149
    anti-submarine 30, 122-127, 149-150, 165
    bombing 34, 36
    'Circus' operations 30
    daylight bombing 16, 18, 25, 33, 60, 121
    dual-control trainers 23
    fighter 34
    long-range day fighter 27
    low-level strafing 33, 36-37
    maritime patrol 30, 38
    night fighter 8, 11, 43, 50
    night intruder 27, 30-31
    reconnaissance 25-27, 32-33
    target-towing 164-166
    training 31
Romain, John 7, 11, 13, 43-44, 53, 95-96, 132
Romanian Air Force 167
Rommel, Gen Erwin 34, 116
Rothermere, Lord (1st Viscount) 18-21, 160
Royal Air Force (RAF) units 18, 20, 27, 34, 159
    Advanced Air Striking Force (AASF) 25
    Bomber Command
        2 Group 30, 121
        204 Group 36
    Coastal Command 30, 142
    Desert Air Force (202 Group) 32
    Fighter Command 27, 29, 115
        1 Group 25
        11 Group 28-29
    Fighter Interception Unit (FIU) 28
    Operational Training Units (OTUs) 30
    13 OTU 31, 163
    54 OTU 30
    10 School of Technical Training 22
    4 Squadron 14
    5 Squadron 36
    8 Squadron 36
    11 Squadron 35-36, 38
    13 Squadron 33, 122-127, 138, 149-151
    14 Squadron 35-36
    18 Squadron 25, 112, 138, 163
    21 Squadron 32, 36
    23 Squadron 11, 27-28, 45, 52, 162
    24 Squadron 22
    25 Squadron 27, 29, 134, 162
    29 Squadron 27, 29
    30 Squadron 23, 31, 35
    34 Squadron 38-39
    39 Squadron 38
    40 Squadron 10
    44 Squadron 23
    45 Squadron 32-35, 39
    53 Squadron 24-25, 163
    55 Squadron 31-34, 36
    59 Squadron 25-26
    60 Squadron 38-39
    62 Squadron 38, 112
    68 Squadron 44
    82 Squadron 36, 159
    84 Squadron 31, 33, 35-36, 38-39
    90 Squadron 23
    101 Squadron 20-22, 111, 158
    105 Squadron 25, 36-37, 112
    106 Squadron 4
    107 Squadron 25, 30, 37
    110 Squadron 25-26, 36, 146-148
    113 Squadron 8, 32-33, 35-36
    114 Squadron 7, 23, 25-26, 30, 161-162
    139 Squadron 23, 25, 109, 148
    144 Squadron 23

    203 Squadron 33, 35-36
    211 Squadron 31-35, 38, 107
    219 Squadron 28
    225 Squadron 14
    254 Squadron 44
    600 Squadron 29
    604 Squadron 28
    609 Squadron 28
    612 Squadron 14
    614 Squadron 38
Royal Air Force (RAF) airfields and bases
    Aden 32, 35
    Alor Star, Malaya 38
    Bétheniville, France 25, 148
    Butterwrth, Malaya 38
    Catterick 28
    Coleby Grange 27
    Collyweston 27, 45
    Condé/Vreux, France 26
    Debden 29
    Digby 27
    Dyce 142, 147
    Egypt 33, 35, 37
    Habbaniya, Iraq 23
    Hawkinge 162
    India 38-39
    Iraq 32
    Java 38
    Luqa, Malta 116
    Ma'aten Bagush, Egypt 32
    Malta 36-37
    Menidi-Tatoi, Greece 31, 34, 107
    Middle Wallop 28
    Mosul, Iraq 31
    North Weald 29
    Odiham 25, 163
    Poix, France 26
    Singapore 38
    Souk-el-Arba, Tunisia 122, 129, 149-151
    Sumatra 38
    Tangmere 28
    Tengah, Singapore 38
    Wattisham 25-26, 146-148
    Watton 159
    West Raynham 158
    Wittering 27
    Wyton 23, 161
    Yelahanaka, India 39
Royal Canadian Air Force 42, 164-165
    404 Squadron 106-107, 137, 142, 147
Royal Hellenic Air Force 167
Royal Navy 36
Royal Yugoslavian Air Force 167

Safety equipment 130
Scarf, Pilot Sqn Ldr Arthur 38, 112
Scivier, Wg Cdr 116
Short
    Singapore 32
    Stirling 30
Smith, John 'Smudge' 44, 129, 131-133
Smith, Cpl M. 142
South African Air Force 167
    15 Squadron 36
Spare parts 42, 130
Suez Canal 31
Supermarine Spitfires 12-15, 26-27, 28, 162

Tail unit 49, 61, 70-71, 135
    elevators 49, 70-71, 81-83, 108-109, 137
    fin and rudder 49, 70-71, 82, 106, 108, 137
    tailplane 49, 70-71, 134, 137
    trimming tabs 71, 79, 82-83, 106, 109, 137
Take-off 19, 29, 98, 106, 127
Taxying 97, 103, 105-106, 127
Tedder, AVM Arthur 34-35

Theatres of operation
    Albania 34
    Bay of Bengal 39
    Burma 38-39
    Crete 35
        Malème airfield 35
    Desert War 35-36
    Eastern Front 36
    Egypt 34
    Far East 37-38, 112, 163
    Greece 34-35, 167
    Italy 32-33, 36
    Libya 32, 37
    Malaya 38
    Malta 36-37, 116
    Mediterranean 37-38
    Middle East 37-38, 112
    North Africa 34, 36-37, 163
    Russia 166-167
    Senegal 166
    Sicily 37
    South-East Asia 38-39
    Syria 166
    Thailand 39
    Tobruk 36
    Tunisia 38, 166
    Western Desert 32-33, 35-36, 166
    Yugoslavia 35, 166-167
Thorburn, Flt Lt 124
Tools and working facilities 130-131
Towing 131
Trenchard, Viscount 19
Turkish Air Force 167

Undercarriage 46, 48, 52, 71-73, 75-79, 110, 131, 135, 137, 140, 153, 162
    Edo floats 164
    lights 104
    main wheels 75-78, 131, 134, 142
    parking brake 103
    retraction 89, 98-99, 106, 109
    safety locks 77
    tailwheel 61, 70, 78-79, 131, 153
    tyres 77, 79, 169
    warning devices 78
    wheel brakes 23, 77-78, 89, 91, 97-99, 104, 141-142
Uwins, Chief Test Pilot Cyril Frank 19-21, 24

Vichy French 33, 166
    Palmyra airfield 33
Vickers
    Vincent 31-32
    Wellesley 32-33
    Wellington 25, 30, 34
Victoria Cross 36, 38-39, 112, 163

Warner, Graham 43-44, 94, 132, 173
Wavell, General 33
Westland
    Lysander 14, 32
    Wapati 32
Williams, Sgt 116
Wings (mainplanes) 22, 46, 48, 71-75, 133-134, 136
    ailerons 49, 71, 73, 75, 79, 81, 109, 137
    covering 72
    flaps 19, 49, 74-75, 83, 89, 98, 106, 109-110, 131, 137
    landing lamps 72-73
    leading edges 50, 72
    navigation lights 73
    spars and booms 72-74, 83
    wingtips 75
Wireless operators/air gunners 61, 67-69, 106-107, 111, 127, 149, 165
Woodhouse, AC A.E. 137

1,000-bomber raids 30-31